I0758176

Sorority of Bereaved Mothers:
*poems and stories from Black Women
on pregnancy loss and infertility*

sorority of bereaved mothers

poems and stories from Black Women on pregnancy loss and infertility

Edited by Camari Carter Hawkins and October B.L.U.

Sorority of Bereaved Mothers
© 2024, Camari Carter Hawkins and October B.L.U.
ISBN (hardcover): 979-8-9893829-4-1

Published by Mama's Kitchen Press
Austin, TX / Los Angeles, CA
mamaskitchenpress.com

First Trade Paperback Original Edition, 2024

Printed in the United States of America

Edited by Camari Carter Hawkins
Editorial Judge: October B.L.U.
Layout Design by Krystle May Statler
Cover Design by Emily Anne Photons and Krystle May Statler

For women in waiting, in loss,
in grief, in hope,
in receiving.

Contents

A Note from Camari

Dear Reader,

I write this from a place of waiting, questioning, long-suffering, and hopefulness.

In 2019, I experienced a miscarriage and have struggled with fertility since then. When I was in the weeds of this fresh trauma, I was hard-pressed to find other women in my close circle who could relate. It wasn't until I became vocal about my experience that other women came forward and said, "Me too, I feel your pain."

Now that I am still waiting on my miracle, rainbow child, this journey presents a separate set of challenges, questions, deep longing, and angst. I am entering my perimenopausal stage in life, and I have seen many women and caregivers deliver children. I am a godmother to the best twins anyone could ever meet. I am the only aunt to my first nephew. I am *Auntie Mari* to my best friend's children. In a way, I see myself as a second mother to these sweet babies. And yet, it hurts like an insatiably hungry void in my soul.

From personal experience birthed a desire to craft this book.

1 in 4 women experience pregnancy loss. That number jumps dramatically when Black women are involved. Oftentimes, we do not receive proper medical care, face financial disparities, and encounter daily stressors and microaggressions that make living in this beautiful body and carrying life a challenge.

These stories within also include voluntary loss and how that, too, never truly leaves you. Either regretted or not, the jolting pain of once carrying life, being a part of something bigger than you, to now getting adjusted to life without can be jarring. This book tackles that sorrow as well.

It is taboo to talk about such darkness. Adding the nuance of spiritual belief, it is easy to cast your care off to your God, your source, your belief, and leave it there. But is it really gone? Is it that simple to endure life-altering pain and forget about it? I don't think that we forget. I also don't think we dwell on it each day. I believe that these experiences mark a dandelion tattoo on our spirit. A sign that we are still here even as the wind carried parts of us away. We remember and we heal.

The stories in this book are written by everyday Black women who have experienced a precious loss that has stayed with them. It was important to me to include stories from women who aren't career writers. These stories have been plucked from the heart of women you'd casually stand behind in the checkout line, walk by in the park, or sit at the stoplight next to. It was imperative that we capture these relatable stories from them. This book and stories offer a safe space to feel seen, heard, and eventually lead to your own personal healing.

While this offering does not aim to provide answers or diagnoses, we aim to offer open arms and comfort through shared stories. Here at Mama's Kitchen Press, we believe that storytelling affirms our humanity. We hope you feel affirmed by the end of this book.

In community and rainbowed hope,
Camari Carter Hawkins, founder of Mama's Kitchen Press

A Note from October B.L.U.

Dear Readers,

My story is one of loss, a journey marked by numbness and body confusion. I found myself laboring a baby I knew had already left this world 48 hours prior. A miscommunication led to a warming bed being wheeled into my room while I slept, only to awaken to the stark reality of my grief.

I share this deeply personal experience with you because I want you to know that you are not alone. This journey is a lonely, longing, and crowded roads, but when you find the strength to raise your head, you will discover extended arms and understanding eyes ready to share space with you. This body of work is heavy weighted with women who understand your pain and are ready to share space with you as you reanimate your wholeness. We will not tell you when enough is enough, but we will offer our unwavering support as you find your way.

With love and solidarity,
October B.L.U.

sorority of bereaved mothers

My baby, you will always be
even if you couldn't stay with me

—Leah Jealene

Even if

Leah Jealene

Words fail me at the sight of my empty womb
Where did you go, little one?
The joy we felt with those bold lines
Our September and Sapphire blue
The anticipation of your first movements
The first moments with you
All swept away
There will be no more appointments
No more updates of your growth on an app
No more expecting what to expect
Our souls met only briefly in another life
With yours, now only in my dreams
I ache as what would've been your safe haven
Slips from my body, leaving behind a vacancy
Will it be filled again?
I don't know that any more than I know
what your first word would have been.
Or your favorite color.
Or who you would've grown up to be
I do know that I love you and wish that you could've stayed.
That I could've gotten the chance to hold your hand
To kiss your boo-boos
See the world through your eyes
To feel your brown sugared skin
To hear you laugh
To be your guide and watch you grow
To hear your "yes," when I said, "no."
My baby, you will always be

Hope and Healing After A Miscarriage

Christina Smith

My journey to motherhood was not easy. Like so many other women, I have survived a miscarriage. Before my first pregnancy, I knew miscarriages happened; I just naively assumed because I was healthy and young, it would never happen to me. I had no idea how common it really is. Miscarrying feels like a secret society that you don't learn about until you are smack dab in the thick of it, and then others open up and reveal they've survived it with you as well.

Our Story

It was spring break, and my husband, Alex, and I were vacationing for a week in the Dominican Republic. On March 30, 2018, we learned that I was pregnant while we were still there. It was one of the happiest moments of our lives! We immediately carved out a special place for our little ones in our hearts and our minds. We began to dream and plan what life would be like for the three of us. A week later, my doctor confirmed that I was six weeks pregnant. We told a few close friends, family members, and our pastor. I continued to imagine what our life would be: like sleepless nights, decorating the nursery, the warm cuddles, the loud cries, and rocking our baby to sleep. We fell so deeply in love with our precious baby. A few weeks later, at our second prenatal appointment, I knew something was wrong when the doctor spoke casually and then fell silent as she performed the ultrasound. After what felt like an endless pause, she finally told us, *"I can't find a heartbeat."* A tsunami of grief crashed over the both of us. We questioned, "WHY, Lord?"

Miscarriage is death. It is a loss unlike any other. It is impossible for me to fully describe what it's like to have someone you love die on the inside of you. I felt like my body betrayed me and failed my unborn child. I wrestled with the idea that it was somehow my fault. I spiraled into over-analyzing what I ate, drank, and what activities I did in the weeks before our loss. But the truth is, it wasn't my fault, and if you've experienced pregnancy loss, know that it wasn't your fault either. For the days, weeks, and months afterward, it felt like a dense fog of deep sadness set over me. I wondered at work if colleagues could see beyond my empty smile. A smile that was desperately attempting to mask immense pain. Could they hear the shallowness in my laughter? Could they tell my eyes were fighting back tears? Could they sense my mind was drifting in mid-conversation, thinking of my lost baby?

Miscarriage is lonely. For something that is so typical, it is so rarely discussed, which makes it taboo and adds a layer of shame to the experience. After a quick internet search, I learned that 15-25% of all pregnancies end in miscarriage. Most people who have not experienced it do not know how to respond. Be prepared to show grace to others who may accidentally hurt you. We had to forgive several insensitive questions and comments. But once I shared with a few trusted friends, I learned some incredible and painful stories of women who survived multiple losses, late miscarriages, ectopic pregnancies, and infertility. These friends prayed and cried with me. I knew I was not alone.

Healing

It took 10 days after that appointment for my body to realize that my baby was no longer alive inside of me. 10 days of waiting for my body to empty itself. That day, I felt God give me His peace. It has never felt more real to me in my entire life. He reminded me that He is close to the broken-hearted and will carry me as I carry this vacancy in my heart for the rest of my life.

I buried myself in scripture. I knew I wanted to have a child again and as soon as possible. I was encouraged by the stories of women in the bible who struggled with pregnancy—the story of Hannah, Rachel, Rebecca, Sarah, Elizabeth, and Manoah's wife.

I'm blessed to say that five months later, my husband, Alex and I found out we were expecting again! On May 16, 2019, I gave birth to a healthy baby boy, Josiah. Which means, "The Lord has healed." I love my son with everything in me, and I am so grateful for him. But children are irreplaceable; BOTH of my babies have their own special place in my heart.

If you have a friend or family member who has experienced a pregnancy loss, here are a few simple ways you can support them:

1) Listen. My friends who really helped me are the ones who simply listened. They sat in the silence, in the awkwardness, in the pain with me. Don't try to explain why it happened; don't offer a hopeful cliché, "You can always try again" or "Everything happens for a reason." Just be present with her.

2) Check in on her (or them). Call, text, reach out in some way, and see how she is doing. Men can also feel deeply saddened by a miscarriage, so if she has a partner, don't assume he isn't mourning also.

3) Show that you remember and care. We shared and prayed with a married couple from our church about our loss. They remembered our due date and gave us a thoughtful card in November. It meant so much to me that someone was still thinking of us and remembering our first baby.

4) Share this. Let them know that they are not alone.

If you have survived pregnancy loss, I encourage you to share your story with someone you trust. They may have even gone through it themselves and have not shared about it. Like most grief, it never fully goes away. It evolves, and it becomes less raw. ***Know that you are not alone. Know that I am praying for you sis. Know that you may have never got to hold your baby in your arms, but you did hold your little one in the most intimate place a person can be held, on the inside of you***. I *LOVE* my first baby more than I would have ever imagined. To love someone so deeply but to have never met them is the remarkable love and pain of motherhood.

I Am

Chelsea Evans

While some of you may be wondering what that may mean, there's a woman out there who has experienced a loss and has suffered in silence. 1 in 4 women have experienced a miscarriage.

The thought of having a living being inside of me and then having nothing at all is painful. I know where my strength comes from, but hearing the words "I'm so sorry, Chelsea, there's no heartbeat" made me angry inside, and it left me so weak.

I am 1 in 4.

This grieving process is truly a hard season for me. Some days I feel like I'm moving forward, while other days,; not so much. I'm just mad. But then I wonder, who can I be mad at? Now, I know that we've all heard that we aren't supposed to question God, but who exactly came up with this rule? If He can handle all of my emotions, couldn't he handle the frustrations and the uncertainties of my life?. Let's be real: I questioned God in this season. But do you know who also questioned God? My Jesus.

I am 1 in 4.

My God, My God, why have you forsaken me?!? Is this some sort of cruel joke? Do you think this is funny?! Because it's not, and it hurts. But God, not my will, but your will be done. I'm reminded that God is getting all the glory in spite of me. And for that, I'm truly grateful for this journey.

Thank you, God, for choosing me to mother this beautiful angel.

I Threw it Straight in the Trash

Alyssa Small Layne, MD

A suspicious envelope came for me. Looking at it mingling with the rest of the mail. It looked to be 5x7 inches, and it wasn't the holidays. I flicked away the other fliers, postcards, and envelopes so I would see it better. Yes, this was one of my most feared correspondences. Worse than late bills. Worse than my bloated student loans. I just knew. But I also knew I had to open it to confirm. I tore open a small part of the envelope, a corner, and I peeked in. I could tell what it was without taking the card out. I could tell from the colors. I could tell from the short four words I read. I threw it out of my hand and into the garbage like it bit me. It did bite me. Baby shower invites hit me hard. 2 weeks before the one-year anniversary of my daughter's passing, it hit me hard.

Complications

Niki Billingslea

I don't know this being
This disruptive force trying to come through me
I don't know what his purpose is
I know it's a him. I just know.
All I know is that his dad just bought a bag of weed
but his car window is broke and it's December
And his five year-old deserves a warm ride to school
I think waiting will be better than trying to raise two men
I tell myself this in the waiting room alone

Before, I knew that abortion was the #1
cause of death in the black community
We die before we come through the portal
Other Black women wait with me
Other Black women have reasons for needing
Black babies to wait to come here

We all try to act like that's not why we're here.
We act like our shit is together
and we just dropped in to say hi to our friend, the gynecologist
The doctor says everything is fine
and that there seems to be no complications
I'm impatient because she knows damn well
the complication is one her training cannot diagnose
The complication is that bringing a black child in the world
is to bring someone into this world to suffer exponentially,
and I don't want to see the pain in his eyes
when he asks me, "are we poor" and "why do they hate Black people"

I confidently say I want to proceed
Left in a room to think
What will they do with him?
Will he be thrown away like trash?

Will they sell him in parts to the genetic science industry?
Will he be torn in pieces?
I turn my brain off
I shut my feelings up in an internal vault
I think I chose local anesthesia
I think I remember the sound of the suctioning
I for certain remember feeling as if a part of my soul was being siphoned
because when they wheeled me out, I felt empty
I felt like a hollow shell
A woman from the waiting room looked beat
She couldn't put her pants on
She shook
and then she screamed
She screamed and she sobbed
and it felt like she channeled the feelings
I had trapped away in that ironclad vault
but I couldn't move
I couldn't tell her it would be all
right I didn't know that to be
true

1 in 4

Sonya Gibson-Dixon

A gut-wrenching ache
that has transformed into consuming heartbreak.
Tucked away in the shadows of sentiments
that foreshadow resentment due to a loss understood.

Forever embodied and carried,
emotions and thoughts vary.
Always concealing,
a pain deemed as unappealing.

Initiated into a secret society,
based on shame and anxiety.
The silence of the world is deafening,
to those whose cries can be heard as echoes.

A loss ignored and viewed as nonexistent,
processed in a fragile heart as a hurtful sentiment.
Taken on by those who know no more
about the unique women that make up 1 in 4.

1 in 4 women have embodied identical thoughts,
isolated and confused as they endure infant and child loss.
A story to tell for each internal scar that has derived
from the loss of a child wanted so desperately alive.

Sit quietly and listen to the woman who is near
let her share her story, and do not interfere.
Continued shame and silence, it's long overdue,
help end this stigma; change starts with you.

The First Few Weeks

Fat Black Chick

A silent ride from my hospital bed to the front entrance.
Left to wait for the truck to pull up.
My arms holding only a bag of personal belongings.
The woman in the chair parked across from me struggles
to hold the awkwardly shaped car seat on her lap.
Reality.

How dare the sun rise!
How dare people smile and laugh;
When I'm confined to the cave of my living room
escaping as far as the bathroom to change
the blood-soaked pad and ill-fitting hospital-issue mesh underwear,
a reminder of my reality.

How many days has it been?
What day is it?
What have we eaten for dinner?
When did I last shower?
Never mind, turn on Cheaters, let's just be…
away from reality.

A knock at the door, unprompted by an order for pizza.
The local florist delivers a plant of consolation.
I revel in its beauty, enjoy the two white blooms
eventually, they, too die,
without regard for my care, my joy, or my reality.

I escaped to the back porch for a while,
Felt the sun on my face and the breeze across my arms.
It was such a pleasant experience, I wanted to be swaddled in it.
Then I felt an unknown sensation, and wet spots emerged across my t-shirt.
I retreated back inside to change,
burdened by my reality.

*Thankfully, as more Black voices are heard,
I won't ever be alone.*
—Marenda Bullock Rose

WHAT IF

Marenda Bullock Rose

Clinicians call them chemical pregnancies. A pregnancy that fades as quickly as the blue lines of the test that first confirmed it. There was a life there. And then suddenly, almost without detection, it's gone. Chemical pregnancies are the reason a woman is advised not to test until her period has been late an entire week.

Because it's just better to not have known.

Clinicians will say there's nothing you could have done differently. That there was likely a chromosomal abnormality. That it's better this way. That it's nature's method of quality control.

But after three in a row—March, April, and May of 2019—quality control feels cruel. What's crueler?

No explanation. The dreaded "unexplained fertility" diagnosis. A stepson who serves as a weekly reminder of my husband's ability to produce life with someone else. 10,000 mg of supplements every day.

Smiling despite sorrow (because, of course, black women are superheroes who don't experience emotional or even physical pain). Wondering if I am receiving the best care from providers, the most dedicated attention. Or am I receiving the care and attention reserved for a black woman? A black woman who, by the way, found out her medical record at a local hospital somehow reflected three elective abortions instead of three miscarriages. I wonder how that happened?

Questioning God. Wondering.

Fighting hope. Allowing hope. Having hope. Losing Hope.

Every month.

Then, starting over after Cycle Day 1.

Fighting hope....

Recurrent miscarriages are a nightmare.

What happens then when there are double lines on a home pregnancy test yet again?

First: *Cry. A lot. And not from happiness.*

I shouldn't have taken this test.

Why is this happening again? Why is this happening to me? Why is God doing this? Or at least allowing it?

Ask God directly. Yell to—or maybe at—Him.

I should have just waited to see if my "period" would come on its own or really late. Then I wouldn't have known. Because clinicians say…

Except I've been diligently charting all month. Charting my ovulation, charting my basal body temperature, charting my fertile window. So, I know what my triphasic BBT and one-day-late period mean.

I already knew I'd see a double line. Why'd I take this stupid test?!

Wait, let me analyze and re-analyze my past charts. Just to make sure. Maybe I can find a different pattern. Maybe this test is different.

Is this line darker than the others on this same day past ovulation? Is it lighter? **Maybe this time, it'll stick.**

No. Don't get your hopes up.

Don't get your hopes up.

CRY MORE

I can't handle this again.

What's wrong with me?

There must be something I haven't found yet. Something the doctors haven't found yet. Something rare, perhaps.

Does my body recognize these embryos as foreign?

SPEND AT LEAST AN HOUR ONLINE

I should be tested for every autoimmune disorder that exists, not just the "popular" ones.

Do I have Celiac disease? I should be tested for that first. Gluten-free isn't hard these days.

Ok, what have I NOT tried yet? Strict diet modification. Acupuncture. Uterine massage. L-Arginine supplements.

Crap, I have to work today. I don't want to be around people. Or maybe I should be around people.

What if this is real, and it sticks this time?

No, don't…

But what if it DOES?

Will it even survive? Will I just have a later miscarriage at 8 weeks? 11 weeks? 20 weeks? Stillbirth????

What if every time I get pregnant, the baby dies?

When does this fear stop???

I'll test again in two days and see if the line is darker.

If it's lighter....

DON'T CRY

I have to pull it together and go out into society now. I have to be "all good." I have to walk around people who have no idea I may be in the middle of miscarrying yet ANOTHER baby. I have to answer, "I'm good, and you?" when I'm asked how I'm doing today.

Or, I don't have to do any of that.

I want to tell someone. But then again, I don't. Because if it sticks, I want the pregnancy to be a surprise. And announced later.

Like normal people.

Like people who don't live this nightmare.

What about my faith? Am I doubting by saying "if?" Is that fear? No, I'm a human. Not a robot. This is ok. I'm ok.

I'm ok.

I'll be ok.

Make a plan. What's next? IVF? A more aggressive, more specialized reproductive immunologist? All the natural changes I just thought of earlier?

A plan is comforting. I can do this.

I won't chart anymore. That way, I won't know if this happens again.

Everything isn't in my control. I can only do what I can do. I can't MAKE this happen or stop happening.

I'm ok.

It's not the end of the world. It's really not. It just FEELS wretched. And broken. But….

What if it sticks?

What no one tells you is that if the pregnancy does indeed stick, as my fourth one did, the anxiety and PTSD of infertility rages on greater, more pervasively and more brazen than ever for the next 36 weeks.

For me, that manifested as nightmares, fits of crying, calling my midwife for as little as a mild cramp, going to the ER because "my baby hiccups too much," setting incessant checkpoints—"okay, we made it to…," kick counts upon kick counts. And that's only after I got the courage around 20 weeks in to stop hiding my pregnancy and actually tell someone besides my husband.

Oh yes, did I mention I have a husband? So, let's not forget the nonsensical "I'm black, but I'm still worthy" hoops many of us have grown accustomed to jumping through subconsciously. In pregnancy, that's me turning my car around and returning home because I forgot my wedding band, and I must NOT be seen in public with a big belly and no ring.

Stress.

…because infertility tries to steal the joy of pregnancy.

After many talks with God and intentional, repeated affirmations – my favorites being "new egg, new outcome" and "just because I think a thought doesn't mean it will come true" – joy did eventually come in the morning. My "if this baby makes it" became "when this baby gets here." I was eventually able to breathe, if only for moments.

My son is now 3 years old with 15-month old twin brothers.

Three losses. Three live children.

I managed postpartum anxiety and postpartum OCD; both had a higher likelihood of occurring because of my previous losses and anxiety. I have to browbeat my wild, intrusive thoughts and still post affirmations and bible verses all over my house.

...because infertility tries to steal peace in parenthood.

The effects of recurrent pregnancy losses and infertility are ongoing long after the diagnosis is technically no more.

Therefore, I still "Voice in Fertility" on my blog of the same name. I still wear orange. I still listen and help when others cannot find the joy. Lord knows I've needed – and still need – plenty of help myself.

Even with one of my sons lying in my lap right now as I write this, I am still an infertility ambassador.

And I will always be.

Thankfully, as more black voices are heard, I won't ever be alone.

Things my mother tells me and how my brain interprets

Camari Carter Hawkins

My friend and I both have daughters
My friend and I both have daughters
and no grandkids
no grandkids

No friend in grandkids

What if I never get
What if I never get
Both kids grand

Kids at grand from both daughters

And my lineage stops here
lineage stops here
here, stop lineage
stop

What if no daughter
never gets grandkids
for my friend and I
my lineage, what if
both stops here

Mother's Day Isn't So Happy For Me

JoAnna Pendergrass, DVM

How do you celebrate Mother's Day after two miscarriages and a failed round of IVF? Not easily.

My miscarriages were about eight months apart. The first occurred when I was about six weeks pregnant, and the second when I was almost ten weeks pregnant.

Both losses left me wondering whether I was even a mother. On one hand, I felt like a mother because I had been blessed with carrying life inside of me. But, on the other hand, I didn't feel like a mother because I had nothing to show for being pregnant.

My miscarriages took my hopes of motherhood away from me. My womb was frustratingly and intractably empty.

The failed round of IVF just made things worse. My eggs didn't even fertilize, which made it feel like we were going backwards. Thousands of dollars of hormone injections couldn't get my ovaries and eggs to act right. At least with my miscarriages, my eggs had been fertilized.

After all of this, I dreaded Mother's Day. I just wanted the day to be over. I didn't want to face a day of celebrating motherhood when it had been taken away from me so many times.

Leading up to Mother's Day, I grew tired of seeing commercials with young children or babies because they reminded me of what my husband and I didn't have. We wanted children, and my body kept on saying no. When commercials that had anything to do with motherhood came on, my husband would immediately change the channel so that I wouldn't have to see images that reminded me of our losses.

My sleep quality and quantity got measurably worse the week before Mother's Day. Waking up feeling tired and uneasy suddenly became the norm.

The empty feeling in my belly became stronger. I'd unconsciously rub my belly when sitting on the couch or lying in bed.

My emotions felt like they were on a tightrope, ready to snap at any moment. I was doing my best to hold it together, but emotionally, I was sinking.

By the time I got up on the morning of Mother's Day, I was emotionally spent. Because of the COVID 19 pandemic, I couldn't just hop in the car and go somewhere to take my mind off of things. I felt stuck at home, wondering how I would pass the day.

I got dressed up and put on one of my brooches that I'd bought the previous year to honor my miscarriages. I made myself a delicious breakfast: waffles, eggs, bacon, fresh fruit, and coffee. I turned on some gospel music to lift my spirits as I cooked and cleaned up in the kitchen.

But what else was I going to do? I decided to write a letter to my babies in heaven and post a video recording of me reading that letter.

With that post, I wasn't aiming for a certain number of likes or views. Rather, I wanted to share the other side of Mother's Day, the side where a woman grieves lost hopes and dreams of motherhood. I knew that there were other women out there feeling exactly how I was feeling, and I wanted them to know that they weren't alone.

Mother's Day is difficult when pregnancy loss and unsuccessful fertility treatment leave a big question mark on your ability to have children. The day becomes heavy with memories of what could have been, would have been, and should have been.

I got through it, but with lots of emotions to untangle. I'm looking forward to Mother's Day becoming easier with time.

Unmothered Thoughts or Unmothered Parts

Nadia Hunter Bey

I think my uterus has performance anxiety
Common expectations have become pedestal penitentiaries
Titles that are umbrella and safety for most
Demand that I drown in pittied disability and exclusion's shade

I think my ovaries have been disenfranchised
Mislead to believe that their working improperly is justice and judgment
The staunch flavor of less than a woman rubbed on my destiny like marinade

I think my fallopian tubes have drunk the jungle juice,
ate the pudding and burned my last pair of white cotton panties
Will no longer send eggs to do the float of shame
To be ambassadors graciously sacrificed to cysts and fibroids

I think that the small amount of unidentified liquid in my cul de sac
is the last of the tears my cervix cried before years worth of childless
winters cryo'd her desire to be healthy

We both needed words of hope...
—Alyssa Small Layne, OBGYN

Infertile OBGYN

Alyssa Small Layne, OBGYN

One of my patients came to see me after surgery. She suffered a ruptured ectopic pregnancy. I was the doctor on call and performed her emergency surgery. Unfortunately, because of the rupture and damage, I had to do a salpingectomy—remove her fallopian tube.

She really wants to be pregnant. She wants another child. She had children with a different partner long ago but was in a new relationship. She and her partner really worked hard for the pregnancy that was lost; an extensive infertility work up, fertility-enhancing surgery, and a whole year of trying. This loss was devastating.

In her frustration and grief, she went on about how easy it was to get pregnant as a teenager. She lamented how it feels like her biological clock is beating so loudly and her chances of a pregnancy are slipping away each day. She was very upset and wanted to know how soon she could start trying again.

And there I sat in front of her. I with two fewer children. I with one less fallopian tube. The former owner of a uterus that broke and was removed. I sat with two years more of trying, two years her senior, and still with a dream of motherhood in my heart. I looked at her with true empathy. My lips released words from deep within. "There's still a chance," I said, "Your window hasn't closed. There's still a chance. You don't have to give up or feel defeated. If you want to, we can keep working towards it. There are still so many options!"

As I listened to those words coming out of my mouth, I wondered if they were for her or if they were for me. In that moment, we both needed words of hope.

Your wings were ready, but my heart was not.

Mizuko 03-20-18

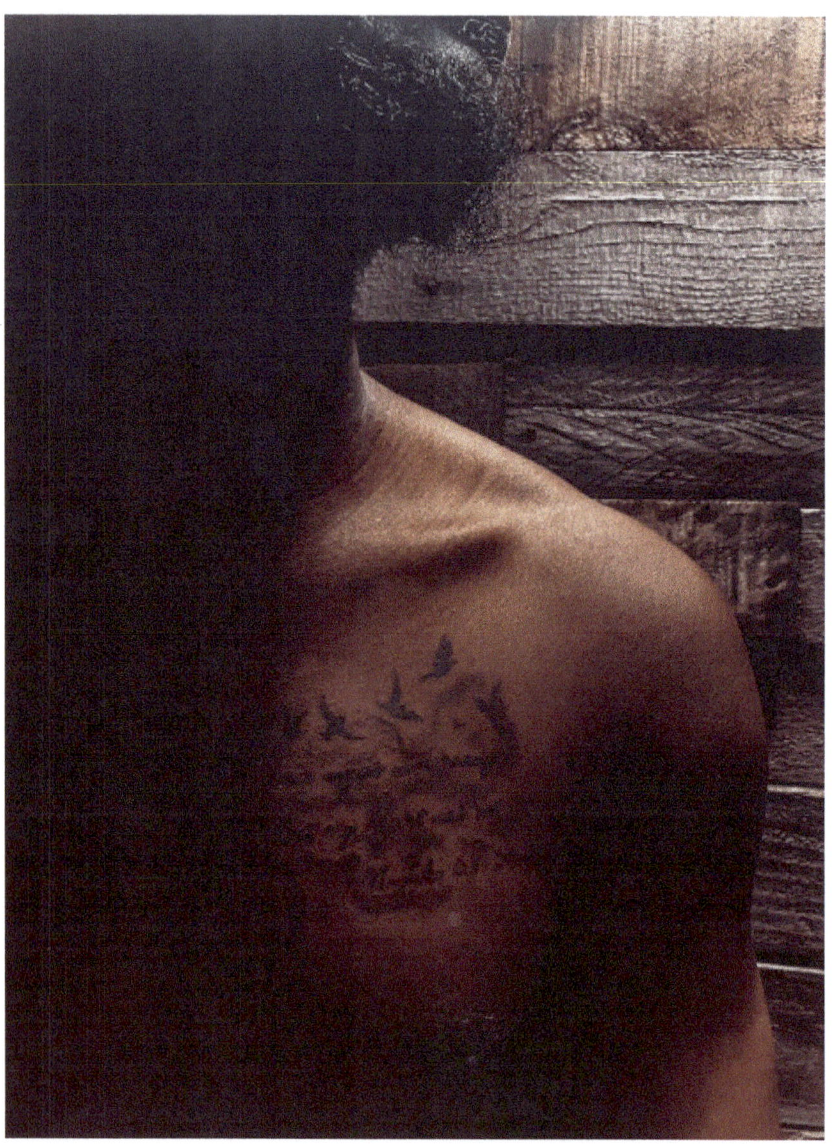

May

Alyse Mencias

By May 2020, quarantine was in full effect. But we were holding on to something special, making the world a little less scary.

Going to a prenatal checkup was the only time I left the house. I put on my N95 mask and said I would video call if I got the chance to see the baby on the ultrasound. I had to go alone to appointments to reduce the spread of the COVID-19 virus.

Starting with the Doppler, the doctor struggled to find the heartbeat, 'no problem, let's get on the ultrasound and take a peek.' I excitedly followed the doctor to the room. The office was mostly empty, calling in patients one at a time from their cars to provide ample space to 'social distance,' the motto of 2020. The doctor was looking at the screen when I pulled out my phone to video call my husband; this first ultrasound of our little guy that he would get to see live. But the doctor stopped me before I made the call.

"I am seeing some swelling here," the doctor said slowly.

"Is it me? Am I swollen?"

"No."

"Is it bad swelling?"

"Yes."

My stomach started sinking.

"I should see a heartbeat here, but there is nothing. There is no heartbeat."

I can't hear the doctor talking anymore. I cried loudly.

The doctor gave me a minute. And showed me, 'It is also measuring too small, around 12 weeks.' The language change stuck out. I know he needed to do this to reaffirm what was happening and to help my mind transition. He needed to be clear and concise. And tell me I miscarried weeks ago.

I drove home in tears, screaming and feeling lost. I'm still not sure how I made it to the driveway. I texted my husband, 'meet me outside, alone.' Our daughter was waiting to hear updates about her baby brother. He knew something bad happened before the front door closed behind him. The doctor made it clear I did not have to go in tonight, but I needed this to be over quickly. I showered and packed a hospital bag. It was too soon for a hospital bag. It was supposed to have a coming home outfit inside. This was not supposed to happen. Why is this happening? I did everything right, right? So many thoughts hung around, just long enough for me to start crying again.

My husband and I took turns being brave and falling apart. We made it through the attempted delivery and eventual D&C. It's a hard place to be when you are grateful for a D&C, so you don't have to be awake while they deliver a child that you'll never meet.

We sat our daughter down and told her about her brother. It was no one's fault, it was nothing anyone did or anything we didn't do. It just was. We told her that she was allowed to feel sad, mad, and confused. She could ask us any questions. It felt like I was saying these words to myself. We cried together as a family.

Then, we started healing together. We had friends and family who hurt with us and helped us recover.

It's been a year since. We never got any answers; just chalked it up to some unknown genetic factor. It still hurts, but I am learning to live with it. We have yet to see another positive pregnancy test. Unexplained secondary infertility, as they call it. What it means is tests, injections, ultrasounds, egg retrieval. It means poor lining, and low egg quality, and sub-fertile and female factor, and it means we waited too long. And if I'm being honest, it fucking sucks.

We have one frozen embryo waiting for us. Our fighter.

Hopefully, we get to meet this person this time.

And that is where we are today, at this moment. Hanging on to new hope. Waiting for new results and letdowns. Wishing for a win.

And in the chaos, we have each other while the calendar shows that it's May again.

At least the quarantine is almost over.

Break Open For Me

Camari Carter Hawkins

Women with open nests for wombs have made me promises
say they'd play nesting surrogate
then pass over young birds to me
and I am to smile
Fetch food
Vomit into their bird
call it mine,
even though its wings aren't like mine
blood not sensitive like mine
beak not sharp like mine
nothing like **mine**

Yet—
give thanks
because these mama birds are so willing
to break open their bodies
for me
when all along, I want my own nest
have a baby ***hawk ins***ide of me

Mother's Day Note

Nadia Hunter Bey

Sometimes flowers don't fit in your bereavement bag
Thank you's are breaths that forced themselves through your experience
Heartbeats keep time to remind you each moment matters
I will not let your dismount become the only elephant in the room I don't
    acknowledge with love

I have fed this season my comfortability
Laid my wishes and regrets on the altar as gratitude and currency
Praying it will be enough

Motherless children deserve flowers and hugs
Everybody knows that
Childless mothers get side-eyed and ignored, patronized for being sensitive
    about something no one ever has the stomach to talk about
Everybody knows that

Except her body
Still calling for a birth and closure to a process that feels like nevermind
    with no reboot
Witnessing hugs and giggles that will never be that personal should not be
    stakes to the heart
But how else will this vampire die

I keep thinking that if I can learn to love myself, then maybe it'll happen
Maybe I'll be considered good steward enough to have a tangible opportunity
That is not just felt or whispered about

A little body that will grow inside of mine
Take over and then move out healthy and whole
All parts fully developed and intact
Someone who will love me because we grew together on the inside

Mother's Day is a sticky variety of wonderment and horror
Depending on how your experiences direct your narrative
What kind of support is expressed
Not all good intended thoughts, words, and deeds feed the right parts
    of one who's still filling their cracks with gold

I am sending this Mother's Day note to all who have ever been on any
    side of motherhood
Allow those who need to be loved differently the space to navigate in
    the healthiest ways possible
Honor challenges and various healing styles
Handle each other with love and consideration
Let's birth real family connections
Where truth, trauma, and healing can all be discussed

Playing God

Marenda Bullock Rose

—Black People Don't Do That. Just Pray About.—

I was raised Christian. Not just Christian, but *Christian* Christian. Like church every day of the week, tambourines and big hats, break in your shoutin' shoes Christian. And I proudly remain a practicing Christian to this day. I love my people – the blacks and the saints – but sometimes, we have a real challenge with God and science.

Yes, God AND science. There is no God vs. science. God created everything. Every material, every element, every atom. Science uses materials, elements, and atoms to make things happen. Therefore, God created science. Done.

However, for some reason, when it comes to fertility—specifically in vitro fertilization (IVF)—and mental health (didn't you know black people don't get therapy), people seem to struggle with this notion of "playing God." Undergoing IVF is no more playing God than undergoing a knee transplant or heart surgery. Or shoot, wearing glasses. After all, those are also medical conditions corrected by science. What makes IVF or fertility assistance any different? That a life results? Well, that's what happens when the medical condition of infertility is treated.

—Oh, Unless You Forget That Infertility Is A Medical Condition.—

Then, I suppose, it's easy to separate infertility from, say, heart disease. But no, the 40% of male infertility factors—such as impaired sperm motility or count—and the 40% of female infertility factors—such as diminished ovarian reserve or blocked fallopian tubes—are biological, just like astigmatism for the glasses-wearer. And the 20% of unexplained infertility is just as biological as Type 1 Diabetes or any other ailment that one didn't sign up for but has to deal with.

Let's go ahead and address the small percentage of infertility that is caused by human factors and could have been prevented. Should a person with lung cancer not be treated simply because he smoked and "brought it on himself?" Of course not, that'd be ridiculous.

So, we're done with that. Or at least, we should be. I don't want to hear any more confusion about infertility being some stand-alone no-treatment-deserved death sentence.

—What About The Bible?—
Let's start with the fact that every reference to children in the Bible is positive, as though having children is something to desire. So clearly, children themselves aren't the issue. Well…they're not an issue as it relates to fertility and conception anyway. They are quite loud and expensive. And loud. But that's a different essay for a different day.

So, Christians, I beseech ye, what did Jesus himself have to say about medical interventions?

Simple.

In the book of Luke (who was a physician, by the way), Jesus explains to the Pharisees why He communes with people the Pharisees felt were unsavory sinners. Jesus' response to them was this:
And Jesus answering said unto them, they that are whole need not a physician; but they that are sick.
Luke 5:31

In other words, healthy people don't need doctors. Those who are not well are the people who need doctors. Of course, this was an analogy to help the Pharisees understand Jesus' point. However, the example He used is key. Jesus endorsed those in need of medical care receiving that care. This analogy is repeated again in Mark 2:17.

Can we be done with this God vs. Science debate now? For these two simple reasons:
- Infertility is a biological medical condition.
- Those in need of medical attention seek help from doctors. Even Jesus said so. That is all.

Now, let the church say amen.

"I don't know what God you believe in, but MY God is all-powerful and cannot be tricked by science into creating a child. If it's not meant to be, it won't work. If it does, you better believe He had a hand in it. I hope your God didn't just hear you underestimate him like that!" —Anonymous

Journey of Hope: Love, Marriage, and Overcoming Infertility at 40

Samantha Fitts, Ed.D.

Are you living the life you envisioned? When I was in my mid-thirties, I began to self-reflect, and I asked myself the following question: Am I living the life I envisioned? I also reflected on the following childhood questions: What do I want to be when I grow up? What are my goals in life? By the time I was 35 years old, I had already checked off many of my answers: Earn a college degree? Check. Become a teacher? Check. Live in a big city? Check. Drive a nice car? Check. Live in a two-story house? Check. Marriage? Well, not yet. Have children? Okay, there was definitely no check for this question. It's funny, but I guess you can say I wanted the fairy tale, the one in which everything falls into place at exactly the right time.

There are some women who don't have a desire to get married and have children, and that is okay. However, I was not one of them. Many women in their late 30s and early 40s postpone marriage or childbearing to obtain their education, establish their careers, and become financially secure. Unfortunately, this sometimes leads to difficulties in finding Mr. Right or conceiving (or both). This can be an arduous and heartbreaking time of life, when it seems lifelong hopes and dreams of family may not be possible. I delayed marriage after pursuing advanced degrees and establishing my career—not entirely by choice since my mate hadn't entered my life sooner. At times, I wondered if it would ever happen.

The road has not been a smooth one. Yes, I wanted a fairy tale, the one in which everything falls into place at exactly the right time. However, fairy tales can sometimes be frightening, too, with gremlins, monsters, and evil witches. The dating scene in Atlanta was challenging; however, I was blessed to meet my husband online at the age of 34, and we married at the age of 36 in September 2011.

I was 36, married, and we were ready to start having kids right away. My biological clock was ticking loudly. I thought that it would happen naturally, just as it was happening for so many people Elroy and I knew.

Throughout the fall of 2011, we didn't take extraordinary measures to conceive since we didn't think they were necessary. When I didn't become pregnant, I thought maybe it would take a little bit longer for us. It wasn't unprecedented, so there was no reason to panic. I continued to pray and had faith God was going to answer my request.

In May 2012, I turned thirty-seven, but I still wasn't pregnant. My biological clock was ticking louder and louder, and now friends, family, and co-workers always seemed to be asking if and when we were going to have a baby. Many also offered helpful advice. The words I kept hearing were, "just relax." Over and over again, the words kept coming: Relax, relax, relax. Don't worry. It'll happen. You're trying too hard. They all meant well.

During the summer, I saw my gynecologist, Dr. Sunny, and we discussed my goal to have children. He stated that if I had not conceived by the following summer, then I would be considered medically infertile. At the end of a year, he said he would prescribe fertility drugs if I were not yet pregnant. Even though I was ready to get pregnant, I didn't want to take any fertility drugs, which can often cause multiple births—I didn't want to be the next Octomom.

So, instead, I started to research ways to improve fertility naturally. The literature stated that getting pregnant was more than just making love at the right time of the month. I had been getting acupuncture, acupressure, and reflexology massages at the mall because they were relaxing, but I came across articles that said these treatments could also enhance fertility. In the fall of 2012, I continued to get reflexology and acupressure massages since the literature said that stimulating certain neural pathways in the body would increase the chances that I would conceive. I figured my body just needed a little extra help because of my age.

And then, finally, in January of 2013, I missed my period and felt different physically and emotionally. I just knew that something was different about my body. Could this be the moment I'd been waiting for? I went to the drugstore to buy an over-the-counter pregnancy kit. I came home, took the test, and watched two blue lines appear. I was pregnant! It had taken a little longer than expected, but Elroy and I were elated. I made a doctor's appointment for my first prenatal appointment. I was only seven weeks along, so Elroy and I agreed not to tell anyone for three months since most miscarriages happen during the first trimester.

When I woke up on a Tuesday morning in early February, I noticed that I was spotting. Now, spotting is not uncommon during pregnancy, but it can also be an early sign of an impending miscarriage. I called my doctor's office, and the nurse told me to come in if the bleeding got worse.

I felt fine, so I went to work. But when I later visited the restroom, I saw more blood, along with some clotting, so I drove to Grady Memorial Hospital, and yes, I was planning to eventually have a Grady baby! After arriving at the ER, the doctor examined and drew my blood. The doctor soon returned and reassured me that I was indeed pregnant.

They next gave me an ultrasound. During the procedure, however, the doctor said she couldn't see the amniotic sac and said that I had probably miscarried. She used the word "probably," which left room open for hope. She then told me to go home and schedule a follow-up appointment with my doctor. Despite her "probably," I knew in my heart that I'd miscarried. And sure enough, when I visited my doctor three days later, my HCG levels—the hormone that indicates pregnancy— were low and only getting lower. I had miscarried.

The next few days were dark. I was devastated because Elroy and I had wanted a child so badly. I was thirty-seven years old and wasn't sure if I could get pregnant again, and even if I could, would I be able to carry the baby to term? I cried, prayed, and asked God, "Why me?" Hadn't I been a faithful servant? Wasn't I living a good life, working hard, and attending church? Again, it seemed like everybody around me was having children, so why couldn't I?

Despite the bad news, my OB/GYN was optimistic when I saw him again. In fact, he rejoiced that we had had a miscarriage. He told me that the miscarriage could be seen as a sign that we could actually get pregnant. "You had an opening!" he said to me, referring to the fact that my fallopian tubes were open. According to him, if I could get pregnant once, I could get pregnant again. Because of his confidence, I was ecstatic that my dream hadn't died, and I tried to frame the miscarriage in positive terms, and in time, I was able to move on.

That spring, I turned thirty-eight, but the inevitable passage of time didn't upset me. It wasn't a question of if but when. We knew that our positive attitudes were the key to getting pregnant again. And last, but not least, I knew from Dr. Sunny's reaction to my miscarriage that there was nothing wrong with my body. As part of being proactive, I tried acupuncture, acupressure and reflexology again. But that wasn't all I did holistically. In July, I also tried vitamin injections. The treatments were expensive, so I discontinued them after a month.

In August 2014, I made an appointment to see Dr. Sunny, my OB/GYN, for my six-month check-up following my miscarriage. It had also been a year since he said that if I hadn't become pregnant by the following summer, then I would be considered medically infertile. He also said that if I were still not yet pregnant at the end of a year, then he would prescribe fertility drugs. When I arrived, I found out that Dr. Sunny had left the practice. Instead, I spoke with a new female doctor, and shared my discussions with Dr. Sunny, and she prescribed my first round of a drug called Clomid. Clomid is used to treat women who may not ovulate regularly, which was the case with me, or who may no longer release eggs. I was reluctant to take the drug since I was still worried about becoming the next octomom, but I didn't want to neglect conventional medical treatment, so I took it. I resolved to use every tool at my disposal.

September was our second wedding anniversary, and we went to Washington, DC. We also went to the baby shower for one of Elroy's friends in nearby Maryland. My heart ached for my husband since all of his friends had children—some even had grandchildren—and here I was, struggling to conceive. As I looked around the reception room, I blamed myself and thought that maybe it would have been better for him if he'd married someone younger, someone who wouldn't have had trouble giving him a child. Like most men, he wanted a son. But I recalled our wedding vows that we would care for each other through sickness and health. I also realized that I wasn't giving Elroy enough credit for his understanding and patience. He may have been frustrated, but he was very supportive of my efforts and stated that we still had plenty of time. Despite being on Clomid, I still hadn't gotten pregnant. After Dr. Sunny's departure, I decided to look for an OB/GYN who was a fertility specialist, and I found Dr. Hastings. He was a renowned fertility specialist with many honors.

After meeting Dr. Hastings on October 11, 2013, he prescribed a second round of Clomid and told me to use ovulation kits. By late October, Dr. Hastings performed an exam to ensure nothing was blocking my fallopian tubes. The test revealed that there were no biological or structural defects that would prevent me from getting pregnant. Good news indeed. Dr. Hastings next checked Elroy's sperm for motility—their ability to swim—and found that Elroy's sample had been completely normal.

November came, and I still wasn't pregnant. I decided it was time to try artificial insemination, technically known as intrauterine insemination or IUI. Dr. Hastings gave me an ultrasound, a new course of Clomid, and an injection of HCG, the pregnancy hormone. Our out-of-pocket costs for IUI and HSG were expensive, but if they worked, we weren't going to worry about the cost. At this point, Dr. Hastings was trying everything short of IVF.

December came, and I still wasn't pregnant. I was frustrated but not defeated. And yet, I still prayed and trusted in both God and my own instincts. My childhood dream for a baby had such strong roots that I just knew I would have a child. We scheduled a second IUI for January of 2014 in conjunction with taking two new fertility medications, Menopur and Femera, which cost over $400 just for the medicine. I was persistent, patient, and prayed, but by the end of February 2014, I still wasn't pregnant. The medications and procedures were all out of pocket and had been very costly, and while I had no problem paying high prices to obtain positive results, pregnancy hadn't occurred. I wasn't giving up! I just went back to where we started in trying to conceive naturally again.

Because the over-the-counter ovulation kits didn't seem to respond to my body, I purchased the OvaCue Fertility Monitor. The monitor was much different than the traditional ovulation kits I'd used. The OvaCue registers changes in a woman's electrolyte levels by simply inserting the monitor onto one's tongue, which thankfully meant no more urinating on a stick. The monitor marks the fertility period for a woman by providing indicators, rendered in various shades of blue, five to seven days prior to ovulation. The monitor costs $400, but it's both sophisticated and simple to use, and it keeps daily track of readings and compares them to readings from the previous month.

It was time to pray more and increase my faith by seeking first his kingdom and his righteousness. There were so many examples of barren women in the Bible who the Lord touched, and his power caused them to conceive.

In Genesis, God promised Abraham that he would multiply his descendants and cause them to become the great nation of Israel when three angels appeared to Abraham and told him that his wife would conceive a son by the following year. However, Abraham was ninety-nine and his wife, Sarah, was approximately ten years younger and no longer of childbearing age. Abraham questioned what they said, but what was God's reply?: Is anything too hard for the Lord?" And, of course, Sarah later gave birth to a son, who was called Isaac.
If God can make an entire universe from nothing, can't he cause a woman to conceive? Of course, he can! I recited these verses frequently, and Elroy and I continued to pray together. I just knew that I would eventually get pregnant. I just wasn't sure when.

IUI hadn't worked, and neither had natural methods. There was still one procedure I hadn't yet tried yet: in vitro fertilization, also known as IVF. Not surprisingly, IVF is quite costly, and I had just one problem: I didn't have that kind of money. The cost for IVF can range from $8,500 to $20,000 plus. In general, the cost of IVF depends on numerous factors, and many websites offer an online calculator to take into account the following variables. In my case, the cost for IVF for me would likely be around $20,000—because I was older, and the older the woman, the more cycles that are used and the greater the cost. Luckily, I found out that there were grants that you could get to help cover the cost, and if anyone needed a grant for this, it would be me.

Despite the risks and the cost, however, IVF can be a very effective way to conceive. I then decided to keep moving forward, and I Googled about finding funding for IVF. In my search, I found the Baby Quest Foundation. The Baby Quest Foundation is an organization that provides financial assistance for women desiring high-cost procedures dealing with fertility, including IVF. The foundation is run by Pamela Hirsch, whose own daughter had fertility issues.

The more I read on the website, the more I was convinced that this might be the right way to fund IVF. But there was just one problem. Part of the application had to be completed by the physician who would actually perform the IVF, and Dr. Hastings didn't handle in vitro fertilization. I called the Baby Quest Foundation, and, to my surprise, I was able to talk with Pamela Hirsch herself. I asked her if it was okay for me to use a certain physician in Atlanta, Dr. Peters, since he also served on their board. Pamela enthusiastically told me that I was free to use Dr. Peters and that he was an exceptional doctor. I was overjoyed. I wondered if Dr. Peters being in Atlanta was just a coincidence or yet another prayer answered. I felt that it was no coincidence. I made an appointment to see Dr. Peters for September 11. In the meantime, I remained optimistic. Before I would see my new doctor, another big adventure lay ahead.

The big event was Oprah's "The Life You Want Tour," which was coming to Atlanta on the weekend of September 5-6, 2014. I needed some additional motivation before seeing Dr. Peters, and this tour would be it. Oprah was touring America to accomplish what she'd been doing on her TV show for so many years: helping people learn about themselves so they can achieve more in their lives. Oprah's tour was a two-day event aimed at helping people adopt a healthier mindset, target what they want out of life, and take the basic steps to achieve it. She toured with people such as Elizabeth Gilbert, author of *Eat, Pray, Love*, Iyanla Vanzant, an inspirational speaker and life coach, Rob Bell, a pastor and motivational speaker, and Deepak Chopra, a doctor, author, speaker, and advocate of alternative medicine. In short, the presentations during the tour were meant to empower people to reach for their dreams by shedding negativity.

All of the speakers, as well as Oprah herself, were powerful and uplifting. I learned about the importance of meditation. Deepak Chopra guided the audience through breathing exercises and meditations. As we inhaled and exhaled, I engaged in visualizations, seeing myself as happy, powerful, and the parent of a child. As I did this, I felt that Elroy and I could attain anything, and we were grateful for the gifts God was giving to us. I have always been an Oprah fan. Attending her workshop and then actually meeting her was an awesome experience. During that weekend, I received the energy and wisdom that so many have felt through her broadcasts. I was more convinced than ever that I could and would have a baby. I was on the right path, and her workshop was a life-changing experience.

Meeting Oprah had been an awesome experience, and now it was time to implement the positive ideas I'd taken away from her tour It was one thing to write down ideas in a workbook while feeling motivated and exhilarated during the actual weekend event, but it was now back to daily life and time to replace any residual negative talk in my mind with positive thoughts and visualizations. Sure, I had already been positive, but Oprah's tour had put my enthusiasm on steroids.

It takes perseverance, and I was "in it to win it," as the saying goes. September 11, 2014, came, and I saw Dr. Peters, explained my case, and told him that I still wanted to have a baby. His center has a world-class staff trained in infertility issues and embryology, and it was located in Atlanta. Was this another sign that God was walking side-by side with me? I hoped so.

But there was a problem. My Body Mass Index, or BMI, was too high for me to move forward with IVF. When a woman's BMI is too high, IVF can be negatively impacted. Fertility doctors often recommend that patients with high BMI lower it through diet, nutritional counseling, and exercise.

After hearing all this, I understood what had to happen before I could undergo IVF. Dr. Peters was very understanding and said that if I could lower my BMI and lose 30 pounds, then I would be a candidate for the procedure. Thirty pounds was reasonable to me. He also told me that since I was determined to lose the weight, he would schedule me for Family Prep Screening. This screening would analyze my DNA—collected from my saliva—to look for rare or dangerous genetic diseases that could be passed to a child. Naturally, the actual analysis of the DNA is expensive.

I underwent the DNA screening in September 2014, and my results came back negative. I contacted a personal trainer and within six weeks, I had lost twelve pounds from working out, detoxing, and changing my diet. I was on my way to my goal of shedding thirty pounds so that I could have IVF. If I stayed on course, I figured I could reach my goal in a few more months. I was as enthusiastic as anyone could be.

After a faculty meeting one day, a teacher, Adrienne, and I were talking about life when she asked, "What are you waiting on to have children?" (Not everyone was aware of my struggles to get pregnant.) I told her my situation, to which she responded,

"You need to take Geritol!"

I was skeptical at first. This sounded like the 'get drunk' advice I had heard a few times before. I needed proof. So far, I found that certain practices increased fertility, such as colon cleansing or massages, but taking Geritol? Come on. When I asked her if she actually knew anyone who'd taken Geritol and gotten pregnant, she said she had. She also claimed it had worked for others she knew as well. Figuring I had nothing to lose, I ran out to purchase some Geritol. I Googled "Geritol and pregnancy." Sure enough, I found dozens of websites and blogs related to getting pregnant after taking Geritol. As I searched, I kept seeing the statement, "There's a baby in every bottle." That certainly got my attention.

I then went straight to the source and visited the Geritol website. The website had a disclaimer that read, "There is, unfortunately, no evidence that taking Geritol can increase fertility or your chances of getting pregnant. We don't make any fertility claims, and we're not quite sure how the rumor got started."

On November 3, I felt too tired to go through my workout routine, so I went home and slept. I figured I was tired because of Daylight Saving Time, which had just happened. But two weeks later, I missed my period. I had experienced irregular periods in the past, but this time something felt different. I felt an unusual stretching sensation in the bottom of my abdomen. I wasn't sure, however, so I told no one, not even Elroy. I needed proof before I shared any news with anyone. Instead of using a home pregnancy test, I went to an Any Lab Test Now center to get a blood test—and I hate needles almost as much as peeing on a stick, but I felt that the results would be more accurate. They told me they'd email me the results the next day. I went home and waited. It had been over three years since Elroy and I had gotten married and started on our baby journey. All I could do was pray and hope: it was all in God's hands now.

When I opened the email the following day, I found out I was indeed pregnant. Finally, it happened, and I had a healthy baby girl in July 2015! Elroy and I are the proud parents of beautiful Nadia Grace, which means hope and gift from God.

My mission is to support and inspire others through my personal journey of going from singlehood to marriage and infertility to motherhood. In my book, *Journey of Hope,* I share my extraordinary journey of hope. You will discover how my faith in God and perseverance led me to the right husband and overcoming infertility to have our first baby at 40. I have had the opportunity to inspire others through radio shows, podcasts, online, and television shows. Back in January 2020, I had an opportunity to discuss my journey of hope with Ms. Oprah Winfrey during her "2020 Vision Tour" during a meet and greet. I thanked her for "helping me get pregnant," and Oprah responded, "I have never been told that before." I further explained that she was a part of my journey of hope by helping me visualize and manifest my desires during her 2014 "Life You Want" Tour."

What sets me apart from others is I developed the courage to speak out and motivate others who have experienced miscarriage and infertility. I am also helping break the silence of African-American women suffering through infertility alone. Unfortunately, for some, there is a stigma associated with miscarriage and infertility. Former First Lady, Michelle Obama recently shared her emotional struggle with infertility, miscarriage, and the use of in vitro fertilization (IVF) to have her two daughters. We must keep the conversation going and encourage women not to feel guilty or ashamed. Infertility and miscarriage affect more individuals worldwide than any of us could ever know.

In addition to women, *Journey of Hope: Love, Marriage, and Overcoming Infertility at 40* is an inspiration for ALL. No matter what you want to "birth" in life you can apply the 4Ps I applied throughout my journey of hope to overcome my obstacles in life.

My 4Ps of Overcoming: Prayer, Plan, Patience, and Persistence:

Prayer. You must pray without ceasing. My husband and I prayed and meditated on the scriptures involving women and men who overcame infertility in the bible.

Plan. You must have a plan. My plan was to get married and have kids. I followed concrete steps to achieve my goals. You still have time to develop a plan in life.

Patience. You must be patient. Life is a journey. I didn't adopt a mindset of defeat. My faith and patience increased through my journey.

Persistence. You must be persistent. Faith without work is dead. I researched, talked to my doctor, applied things discovered, and made adjustments when needed.

I want the world to know you were here.
—Michelle Prejean

You Were Here

Michelle Prejean

It may have only been for a moment,
but I want the world to know
you were here
and as people and time move on
I want to whisper to everyone
don't forget he really was here

Your place in time may not be marked
by first words, first steps, first teeth
but I still want people to know
you were here
you had ten fingers and ten toes
with the sweetest heartbeat I've ever known

Yes, you were here.

The Birth of Life After 2 Losses

Vu-An Foster

My story is not the traditional story of "boy meets girl, girl falls in love, they get married, and live happily ever after." Six months prior to me getting pregnant, I decided to end my relationship with my on-again, off-again high school sweetheart. We were living together for about two years, and I just wasn't happy. We discussed having a family together, and not once did it ever happen. After we had broken up and he had moved out, I decided to do something for myself. I bought another dog, and I wanted to start a business. I did some research, and then I applied for a 12-week program that offers hands-on training in business planning and management at Rising Tide Capital: The Community Business Academy.

One day in class, a fellow entrepreneur sat next to me. We talked about my business idea, and guess what? He loved it! He didn't think it was stupid or weird. He didn't belittle me which was something I was used to towards the end of my last relationship. He told me I should consider making doggie fruit cups. I thought this was a great idea because my dogs love fruit. He drew some little notes in my workbook. I will never forget the feeling I felt. He made me feel like I was in high school again. I even found myself getting into trouble in class with him for laughing and talking.

One day, he left class early. Later, I found out it was to celebrate his birthday, which was the following day. Something else we had in common was both of our birthdays were in May. Leading up to my birthday, we had been inseparable. However, I had not told anyone in my family about him. On my actual birthday, I told him my family was coming to visit, thinking he might get the hint and leave. He replied, "Great, should I buy food for everyone?" Up until this point, I had merely been enjoying myself. The weird thing about it was our connection was so strong that I felt like I had known him for years. He even joked around calling my newest addition to my family his son because he would accuse me of showing favoritism towards my older dog. Unbeknownst to both of us, we were about to have another addition to our family.

Imagine both of our surprise when the two lines appeared on the pregnancy test. It was the 4th of July, 2017, when we found out I was pregnant. I always wanted to be a mom, but I was met with mixed emotions when I saw the positive pregnancy test. I was shocked, scared, and anxious. I wondered if I would be a good mom and if I was ready, as this was not planned. Many of my worries subsided the first time I saw her on the monitor. She was so small she reminded me of a jelly bean, and from that point on, she became our "Jelly Bean." My OBGYN said our due date was March 15, 2018. My pregnancy was normal after that. I went to the OBGYN appointments as scheduled. I also went to Maternal Fetal Medicine (MFM) for my scans. One day, after I got out of the shower and dried off, I noticed water had started to trickle down, and then a whole gush of water came out. I called my OBGYN, and he met us at Labor and Delivery. I was given two options: to terminate, as without the amniotic fluid, her lungs would not develop, or continue with the pregnancy. We decided to continue, and we were counseled on the risk.

A week later, my temperature began to rise, and I started having contractions. I was told I would need to be induced as the pregnancy had become septic and life-threatening. Jelly Bean came to us at 19.1 weeks on October 18, 2018. And my gut instinct was right; she was a girl. It was one of the hardest and most traumatic experiences in my life thus far. At my post-op appointment, my OBGYN wanted me to have preconception counseling at Maternal Fetal Medicine (MFM) to make a plan for my next pregnancy. I secretly booked the appointment and went alone because our first pregnancy was unplanned.

I eventually told him that I now wanted this more than ever. And exactly nine months after we lost Jelly Bean, I had a dream I was with her, and I was trying to put her in something to keep her safe. She said, "No, do not worry, I will be back," and then she disappeared in the dream. I took a pregnancy test that morning, and lo and behold, I was pregnant again. Panic set in almost immediately. I called my doctor, and I demanded to be seen sooner rather than later due to my history. I went in and had my scan. As my scan did not match my last menstrual cycle, one of the OBGYNs in the practice was not quite convinced I was pregnant. Then the head OBGYN came in and rescanned me, and it was determined that I was about 5 weeks with a new due date of March 22, 2019. My OBGYN and MFM specialist had already decided, prior to me getting pregnant, that I would be monitored closely next time.

I saw my OBGYN on a monthly basis for checkups and vaginal swab cultures. We started cervical lengths at 15 weeks to check for cervical changes bimonthly. At my 16 weeks' scan, I asked the technician if it was too soon to find out if she was a girl and, lo and behold, she was. At my 18 weeks' scan, we noticed my cervix began to shorten. I was scheduled for emergency transvaginal cerclage (TVC). I thought we were in the clear, but at 22 weeks, I felt a trickle of water. I called my OBGYN, and decided to head into Labor & Delivery before I received a call back. I attempted to explain that I felt like what happened in my last pregnancy was happening again, but I was briefly checked and discharged. I got to the parking lot by my car, and the remainder of my water broke and mushed out. This time, I was able to maintain my pregnancy in the antepartum unit. At 23 weeks, I went into labor, and "Valentina Marie" was born on November 15, 2018, and lived for over an hour.

I thought the plan we made with the doctors was bulletproof. I did not know it was only an 85% chance that the transvaginal cerclage would get me to 24 weeks. If I had known that, I would have researched other options. Before I left the hospital, the Director of MFM and my OBGYN met me at my bedside and told me there was still a chance I could carry my own children in the future. They also told me prior, they were not 100% sure I had an incompetent cervix, but after having two second-trimester losses, they have now confirmed I do and would be willing to place a transabdominal cerclage (TAC) prior to me getting pregnant again.

Three months after I lost my second daughter, Valentina Marie, I had my TAC placed in March 2019. Now, I have entered a new stage in my life. Life after two losses and patiently waiting for what God has in store for us. And in the meantime, we will continue to make our mark on the world.

Jelly
Bean
Valentine
Marie

*Your words may mean more to her
than you can ever imagine.*
— JoAnna Pendergrass, DVM

Silence

JoAnna Pendergrass, DVM

Everyone is so ecstatic when you tell them you're pregnant. Their excitement jumps through the phone. But then, sometimes, there's silence when they find out you've had a miscarriage. That silence is deafeningly, frustratingly, quiet.

I didn't notice the silence after my first miscarriage. That miscarriage knocked me so swiftly off of my feet that the silence didn't even occur to me. All I could manage was to try to process what just happened to me and my body.

When we announced that I was pregnant for a second time, our friends and family were over-the-moon happy. This second chance at a miracle, as I called that pregnancy, brought immediate excitement and anticipation. But then, when the news spread through the family grapevine that I'd miscarried again, expressions of sympathy were noticeably and painfully absent.

It's not that I expected to get inundated with calls or texts after my second loss. And, it's not like no one reached out to me (thank goodness). What hurt was that there were certain people whom I thought would have contacted me to see how I was doing, but didn't.

Granted, society doesn't teach us how to respond to the news of a miscarriage. How does someone sympathize or empathize with a loss they can't see? What words can you say to a woman who has experienced such a devastating and intimate loss?

It is understandable that people often don't know what to say to provide comfort after a miscarriage, and thus opt to say nothing. However, to the woman experiencing the loss and grieving that her journey to motherhood was cruelly cut short, that silence can compound the grief and open the door for feelings of anger and bitterness.

That was me. Anger and bitterness overtook my spirit, filling me with negative energy. However, I knew that I couldn't stay in this negative space. Writing out my feelings in my journal and talking through them with my therapist and husband, I was eventually able to make peace with the silence.

I decided that I would honor how I felt about the silence while also honoring the decision that others made to be silent. Honoring both sides allowed me to replace my anger and bitterness with grace and peace.

Acknowledging and talking about pregnancy loss is difficult, both for the woman who experienced it and for those around her who know about the loss. If you know a woman who has had a miscarriage, resist the temptation to stay silent. Take the step to say something as simple as "I don't know what to say, but I want you to know that I'm here for you." Your words may mean more to her than you can ever imagine.

Support Squad

JoAnna Pendergrass, DVM

My support system, which I affectionately called my 'support squad,' was integral to my journey through two recurrent miscarriages and IVF. When I think back to my infertility journey, I remember just how lucky my husband and I were to have so many people—friends, family, colleagues, clergy at our church—thinking about us, praying for us, and checking in on us.

There is no way around needing a strong support squad through a difficult infertility journey. You need people who will pray for you when your spirit feels drained from the physical, emotional, and spiritual turmoil of infertility. You need people who you can open up to without fear of judgment. You need people who will focus on listening to you rather than telling you how you should feel. You need people who will prop you up when your journey knocks you sideways and leaves you reeling. You need people who can make you laugh and keep you filled with positive energy.

As I weathered the ups and downs of my infertility journey, I came to value authenticity in my interactions with people. By 'authenticity,' I mean a deeper level of conversation where we can truly open up about what's going on with us and fully tune into what each other is saying. I have come to enjoy, even crave, these authentic conversations. These conversations, without fail, leave me feeling uplifted and full of positive energy.

I am fortunate that several of my friends went through IVF, and their support and insight were incredibly helpful. However, it's not necessary for everyone in your support squad to have been through what you're going through. For my family and friends who hadn't experienced pregnancy loss or fertility treatment, talking with them became an opportunity for me to teach them about those different experiences. Sharing my knowledge with them helped them understand what so many women and couples go through and perhaps even helped them learn how to better respond to another couple's fertility struggles.

After three rounds of IVF, which included two canceled embryo transfers and one successful embryo transfer, my husband and I were blessed with our son. Being on the other side of infertility, I am passionate about supporting other women who are experiencing the same struggle. I want to support them in the same way that I was supported when motherhood felt like it was slipping further and further away from my grasp.

To those of you whose journey to parenthood has been difficult, I say this: Lean on your support squad. If you don't already have one, be proactive about seeking out people who will support you through this difficult time. The more people you have to support you, the better you will be able to weather the storms of infertility.

Emotional Roller Coaster (Haikus)

Alyssa Small Layne, MD

The sun is shining
and my heart feels much sorrow
the blue sky mocks me

Through all my sorrow
the ups and downs, here and there
I stay positive

A Mother's Heart

Sada Frederick

2020 will always be and forever be an unforgettable year for me, and not because of the COVID-19 pandemic. In January 2020, I discovered I was pregnant. I fell in love with my precious baby the moment I saw the positive pregnancy test. The first initial ultrasound at eight weeks went well, strong heartbeat and rising HCG blood levels. I was given an estimated due date of September 19, 2020. I was given a referral to a high-risk pregnancy doctor for my twelve-week ultrasound. Everything on March 13, 2020, just seemed so perfect that day. I was super excited and had even picked out baby names for boys and girls. Little did I know my world would suddenly change the moment I walked into the examination room.

I propped up on the table, belly exposed, ready to see the beautiful blessing that God had gifted me. The minute I looked at the screen, I knew something was wrong. My baby was just lying there. The ultrasound technician was trying her hardest to find a heartbeat, and then she suddenly left the room. The doctor entered the room shortly after and also tried to find a heartbeat, then those awful words came. "I'm sorry, there is no heartbeat." I was told that my blessing from God stopped developing at ten weeks. I was told I had a Missed Miscarriage. I had no signs of bleeding, cramps, and my belly was still growing. I was heartbroken, lost, confused, angry, disappointed, and just all over the place.

I had to snap out of my stupor. I still had two children who needed their mother. My goodness, that was some heavy news. How was I supposed to process this? I had to muster up enough strength to tell my fiancé the news. It didn't work. Every other word was filled with uncontrollable crying. Then, I had to call the doctor's office to schedule a D and C. Once again, this was all new to me. So you are going to suck my child out of me? I was scared. However, my body had other plans.

March 16, 2020, is a date I will never forget. I instantly referenced the Bible verse John 3:16. I went to the Doctor's office that day to finalize my D and C. Later that day, I began cramping and experienced the most excruciating pain as I went to use the bathroom. I knew at that moment my precious baby was leaving my body. It was so heartbreaking, I saw my baby peacefully sleeping in a sac. I went to the local hospital for treatment. I was told to bring my baby with me for testing. I sat in the waiting area of the emergency room for what seemed to be hours. I sat there bleeding heavily, and there seemed to be no sense of urgency by the hospital staff by what was happening to me. Finally, I received a room and was seen by the physician. I was simply given medication for the pain and told to follow up with my physician.

When I arrived home, everything just seemed surreal. l looked in the mirror, and my pregnant belly was no more. Then here comes the part about having to explain to the handful of family and friends I did inform about my pregnancy. I was mentally exhausted, having to keep repeating the news and receiving unsolicited advice. I know they didn't mean any harm, but I don't think people realize sometimes it is better not to say anything and just listen. I was sick of hearing, " I'm so sorry." The symptoms and constant reminders still linger.

For weeks, I had to go back and forth to the doctor's office for ultrasounds and bloodwork to make sure my womb was no longer carrying any remnants of my pregnancy and Hcg levels. The continuous appointments just added more fuel to the fire, especially having to walk into the doctor's office and see pregnant women. Boy, was that a super slap in the face. Of course, I was told the miscarriage was not my fault and that they are very common, but I felt the opposite. I thought did I eat something wrong, lift something too heavy? All kinds of thoughts ran rampant in my mind. The biggest question I had was for God. God, how could you let this happen? I woke up as brokenhearted as I was and acted as if I was okay, but I was dying on the inside.

As I began navigating my healing from the loss of my Angel Baby, I discovered six weeks later that I was pregnant once again. Just like the last pregnancy, I fell in love with my baby the moment I saw the positive pregnancy test. However, I was very scared and nervous because I had just experienced a miscarriage weeks prior. I thanked God for Him blessing my womb once again and prayed that He would let this pregnancy go full term. With each passing week, I prayed and thanked God for letting me continue to carry what I was blessed with. We found out the sex of the baby very early by way of genetic testing. We were having a girl! We decided to name our angel Aaliyah Layona Clarke, we thought it fit her perfectly. The genetic test, however, did reveal that I carried the gene for spina bifida, which I could potentially pass down to Aaliyah, here come the worries again.

I was scheduled to see a Maternal Fetal Medicine Doctor to ensure that Aaliyah's spine was developing correctly. As the ultrasound technician conducted the scan, she uttered that my pumpkin's spine was beautiful. I thanked God I dodged that bullet. Everything seemed perfect, and my doctor set in place a plan to include weekly progesterone shots starting at 16 weeks. I was scheduled for a cerclage on July 20, 2020, which went pretty well. My health insurance provider would not authorize the progesterone shots that were much needed and recommended by my physicians and stated I would have to file an appeal to have the medicine authorized. After multiple phone calls with my insurance provider, they repeatedly stated because I had a cerclage, they were not going to authorize the progesterone shots. So, you mean to tell me I'm paying you out of my paycheck every week, and you have the audacity to deny something I need. That is all wrong.

As my pregnancy continued, everything seemed fine, but I began to experience some spotting here and there, as well as recurrent UTI's. I went to the emergency room and was told I was dehydrated as well as a Urinary Tract Infection. I was discharged and given antibiotics. I scheduled a follow-up with my physician to ensure my UTI was gone. I remember asking the doctor to please make sure my UTI was gone. Her response was, "Didn't the hospital already treat you for that?" I thought to myself, "Wow, okay, I'm making sure you to check because I am your patient, and I'm concerned that the infection is still there. She never checked to see if the infection was gone.

As the weeks continued on, I know I prayed to God to let me please carry my Aaliyah to full term. I had finally received authorization from my insurance provider to begin the weekly progesterone shots. In the month of September, I visited the emergency room and my doctor's office numerous times. On one particular visit, September 15, 2020, I went to the emergency room and was told my cervix was dilating through the cerclage and that it would be best if the cerclage was removed, but Aaliyah would not survive. I was only 21 weeks pregnant. To add insult to injury, the doctor stated that they couldn't do anything to stop my contractions because my pregnancy had not reached 24 weeks gestation and even brought the weight machine for babies inside the room. I refused to accept what I was being told and was given the option to transfer to another hospital for a second opinion. I was transferred and kept overnight for observation, but I was experiencing significant bleeding. I was discharged once again with more antibiotics and was told to take it easy. As the week progressed, the bleeding decreased, and I thought everything was on the up and up, and the cerclage was still in place. I received my first round of progesterone and even had at-home nursing visits set up. Here comes the morning of September 23, 2020, around 3 am.

I was restless the whole night. I used the bathroom a ton of times, and the bleeding had returned. I sat on the toilet and felt so much pressure, I looked down and saw my baby Aaliyah exiting my body. I picked my baby up out of the toilet and placed her in the bathroom sink.
Everything just happened so fast. I recall the 911 operator walking me through the steps in an attempt to save my Aaliyah. I took a pair of tweezers to open the placenta and saw the body of my baby girl. I wrapped her in a towel and started CPR. I saw her chest rise and fall and thanked God for her breathing on her own. The Paramedics arrived shortly after, and Aaliyah and I were transported to the local hospital.

We arrived at the hospital, and Aaliyah was taken to the NICU. I was taken to a room in the maternity ward. Aaliyah was then transported via helicopter to another hospital that handled babies that small. I saw my sweet Aaliyah before she was transported to the high-risk NICU. She was baptized, by the way, and perked up a little with a touch from me. Here I am, sitting in this hospital room alone, mind just all over the place and womb empty. I was discharged from the hospital hours later, and of course, I rushed over to see my baby girl. I walked into the NICU full of hope because Aaliyah had survived the home birth and transport. I sat at her incubator, amazed at what God had gifted to me. Aaliyah was so beautiful as small as she was, weighing 15 ounces and measuring 11 inches. As we sat at Aaliyah's bedside, her vitals started to decline and were not improving.

The neonatologist shared her concerns, and then reality set in, my baby was going not to survive through the night. We had to make the heart-wrenching decision to take Aaliyah off of life support. Her lungs were not developed enough, and she had some brain hemorrhaging. I could no longer stand the sight of the nurses pumping on her little chest as they were trying to resuscitate her or the constant needles they were poking her with. I was keeping her alive for me and only prolonging her agony. The nurse removed Aaliyah from her incubator and allowed me to hold her until she took her last breath. I held her, talked to her, kissed her, and rocked her in the rocking chair. I handed Aaliyah's lifeless body over to the nurse, so she could clean her up to prepare her for the morgue. "Wow, what just happened I was thinking, is this even real? This certainly has to be a nightmare."

The neonatologist wanted to talk to us again, this time about arrangements. The doctor mentioned the free service that was offered by the hospital, cremation with a shared gravesite. "No, ma'am, I don't think so. Aaliyah was my baby, and she will be coming home to be with her parents." Before we left the hospital, we both said our goodbyes once again, and that was the longest ride home I had ever experienced. I remember as soon as I arrived home, I could no longer contain my emotions, and I just screamed and cried all night. I wanted my baby back and literally wanted to die in order to be with her. The next day, I found a funeral home that would assist me with funeral arrangements for my sweet baby girl. I went to the funeral home to sign off on some paperwork, and I was able to see my baby one last time before she was to be cremated. I kissed her and told her I loved her again. She was so cold. Aaliyah looked as though she was sleeping. It was so unnatural seeing my child like that, facing the reality that Aaliyah died, and it was so tough having to repeat the words, "My daughter died."

It was extremely tasking to take the phone calls of those who had heard the news of Aaliyah's passing. I was frustrated with hearing "I'm so sorry", I didn't want to hear anything. My body was still responding and reacting to my pregnancy. I had filled breasts but no baby to drink the milk. On top of that, my hormones were all over the place, and I could still feel fluttering in my empty womb. Over the weeks, I replayed what occurred over and over and went through a plethora of emotions. I know it was by the grace of God that I am here today to tell my story. I was in the darkest of dark places. I would ask God to just let me die so that the pain in my heart could go away. I hated life, my faith had been tested once again. Why does God keep on testing me? Why? Why? Why? I needed some answers. Why did my body fail me? How can this be God's will? God, do you love me? God, why did you choose my child? My follow-up visit was yet another slap in the face.

I was forced to look at pregnant women with their big bouncing bellies, and once again having to regurgitate the horrific experience of how my Aaliyah died. I walked out of the office feeling more empty than when I went in. I was so hopeless. I didn't receive any kind of closure. I received an "I'm sorry" once again. I didn't receive an answer until months later when I went to a new physician. I had an infection in my placenta that contributed to pre-term labor. The bills were a constant reminder: how in the world are you billing me? My baby died. I received bills totaling approximately $70,000 and had to fight with the insurance company to get those paid. I received Aaliyah's Birth Certificate with the word "Deceased" watermarked across the document. Aaliyah's death certificate had also arrived. Those two documents were just another reminder of my reality—Aaliyah had lived for thirteen hours and 38 minutes, her birthday and death date had the same date.

I had days when just opening my eyes seemed like too hard of a task, and getting out of bed was simply too much. All throughout my days, all I could think about was my baby girl, Aaliyah. I replayed the events of her birth daily. Imagine the mental toll of birthing your own baby one minute and then, in the next second, having to give them CPR. Has anyone had to do this before? Whew, that was traumatic in itself. Everything seemed to be triggered, and there were the constant reminders of Aaliyah not being here physically. My body was here on earth, but I was in a really dark place. I was on an emotional roller coaster. I hated life, I had suicidal thoughts, I couldn't deal with my other children, I was just an empty shell. I started my healing journey when I came to a place of acceptance. Aaliyah had died and is now with her Heavenly Father and also her grandmother (my mother) Althea. Aaliyah's Urn is in a sacred place in my home. I make sure I tell her I love her every day.

The hospital gave me a memory box filled with some of Aaliyah's belongings. I open the box during some of my visits, look at her photographs, and listen to her heartbeat. I am so grateful to have those keepsakes, I often tell her that I didn't even get a helicopter ride, and she got one. I made changes to my environment and sought the help of multiple therapists. I could not handle this on my own. I took each day one second, one minute, or one hour at a time. I lost my two babies six months apart, but in the midst, I found myself. I was forced to sit with myself and do the work to become whole. God had gotten my attention, and I discovered that He was the ultimate source to get me through this pain.

Until one experiences the death of a baby, they will never know the true pain that resides in a mother's heart. There is not one day that passes in which I do not think about my babies. I mourn for the future of my babies, the memories and milestones I will never get to experience. Another painful reality for me was that I was a first responder, but could not receive the help I needed that would save Aaliyah. I was the one that people called when they needed help, but when I asked for help, it wasn't taken seriously. I had experienced racial disparities in relation to maternal care for black women. I was pleading for help so many times, but my requests were ignored, and my baby paid the price. I do not want to hear that everything happens for a reason, I'm still looking for that reason. My faith did waver and I found it hard to pray, but looking back, I know God was walking with me all along. We were never promised a life without trials and tribulations. Everyone will experience grief differently, but the one thing I suggest is to give yourself some grace. Take small steps on your healing journey, a small step is still a step. Allow yourself to feel what you need to feel. Please do not suppress your emotions and how you feel.

My healing journey included me intentionally getting in God's presence daily and telling God my true feelings regardless of how ugly they were. He already knew, anyway. To lose a baby takes a different kind of strength to press on. There will forever be a pain in your heart that will never go away. You will indeed be a different person, every day I have to fight to find my light. Ask for help and be truthful with your feelings. I felt as though if I could make it through the deaths of my babies, I could conquer anything. I know that I will see my babies again. I will carry them in my heart forever.

Jeremiah 29:11 has helped me to make it through. "For I know the plans I have for you declares the Lord, plans to prosper you and not to harm you, plans to give you a hope and a future." I will forever and always hold on to my faith and hope no matter what trial I face. The loss of my babies will forever change how I see life. Every day, I take small steps at a time. I just want to remind all of the mothers who have experienced the loss of a baby. You baby mattered, and you still matter. Love Yourself.

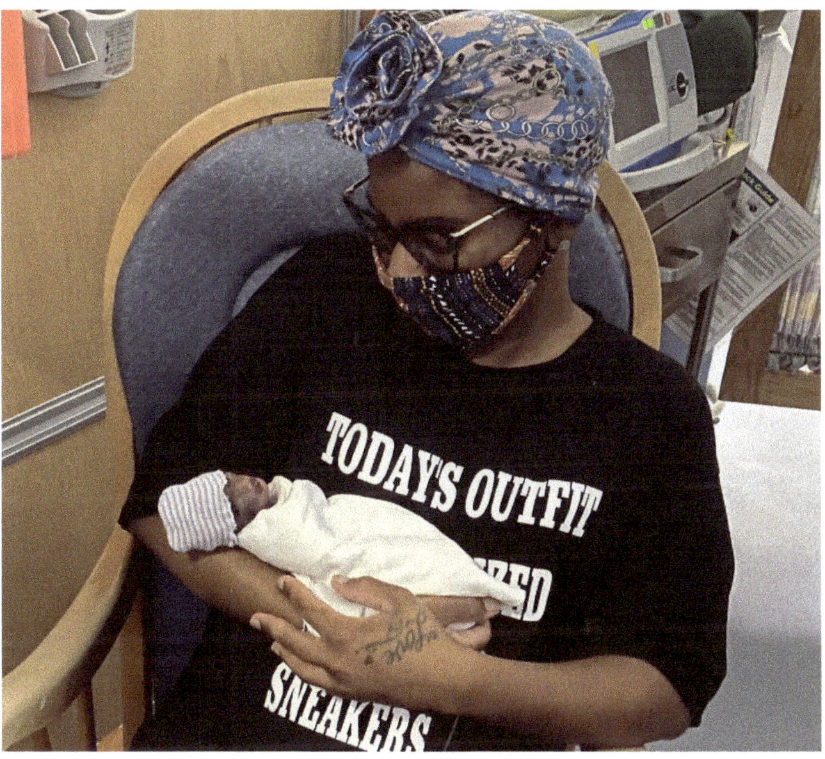

His Still Heartbeat

K. Tilghman

*Deep inside of me lies a scar, a wound that only time can heal. A life innocent…
unaware of the world that awaits him upon his appearance. He moves, kicks, and
turns, as if he can hardly wait to see what adventure lies for him on the outside.*

*His mother, not so innocent, yet still a life unaware of the changes taking place within
her and around her. Confusion, chaos, heartache…Longing to keep the life she has
bonded with, but dreading the life he faces when he finally comes on the scene.*

*Like an earthquake, her body is shaken.
And then the calm before the storm…*

*Silence, stillness in the air, as she searches for the heartbeat that she once dismissed but
now has come to love. It has begun…Is he alright? Where is his heartbeat?
Why isn't he moving…? Subconsciously she knew the inevitable would occur.*

He would return to the Giver of the most precious gift,—Life!

*Sometimes, after acceptance comes loss…
It has happened…She sees his excitement, but she knows the outcome.
She has a choice to make – fight for his life at the risk of losing him in the battle
OR let him go in peace. Of course, she chooses peace over struggle.
…Given the opportunity, she would have given her life for her son's…
But God's purpose for everything and everyone is much greater…*

Don't ever forget that mommy loves you!

06/26/00

Ransom

India DeFINEd Barnes

they send signs of death
weekly
to 85 E. 9th Ave, Apt A
a box, once reception
for evidence of life
signposts for birth yearly
now buried under

twin invoices
silent
demanding
payment
for what she had done

They delivered blackmail
for her failure
to deliver Black Males

a crime fit to bill
her punishment
a moratorium on life and fines
to mock her standard answers
of wellness

She was FINE

not that they checked for her answer
Before they sent death in box A
a reminder of what lied in her womb,
guess they wanted her to pay

she did

every day
she walked to that box
paid respects
to her sons
when she twisted
her key to unlock
the notice of death
in her mailbox
A price she could not afford
but no amount close
to her once pregnant
double conception
loss
A price they extorted
in vain

her children
had already been shipped
to her door in black box
no room in Box A
no bell for this hell
Just ring around the roses
these ashes, these ashes
will never be
what they once were
they're all she has now

so, send your ransoms
there is no negotiating
with terror—it is
they are
She is
already gone

*My wounded womb worries if
you will return one day...*
—Estee Marie

Wondering Womb

Estee Marie

My wounded womb worries if you will return one day
Once uninvited,
you are now welcome
In my selfishness, I cut your visit short.
9 months really isn't long in the grand scheme of things
But 36 weeks seemed like forever
An abrupt insert to 8 week quarters
I was not a math major,
Dividing the time was a skill I lacked
and I could not bear it

My wondering womb now awaits
your return

At lease you have your son

Christina S.R. Williams

Four weeks and seventeen hours after Chloe was silently born, I returned to work. As much time as I had intended to take off, I had bills to pay, and I had a chief who was not very understanding. I found myself in a daze, bracing how my co-workers would react. A few coworkers were kind enough to send me flowers, and a few others sent emails or text messages. Walking into my office building and hitting the elevator button for floor 3, I remembered taking a deep breath and being grateful that I was the only person on the elevator at 6:55 that morning.

Walking into my office suite, it was pleasantly quiet. Most of my co-workers hadn't arrived yet. I began taking the 96 steps from the office suite front door to my office door and was suddenly met with sad eyes. One of my co-workers, whom I had not seen in a few weeks, greeted me and rushed into his office. The sad eyes were already a sign that today, my first day back in the office, was going to be…somber.

After unlocking my office door, I grabbed my cup of coffee and began getting into the groove of things. I logged into my computer and checked hundreds of emails I had received. It was a much-needed distraction until more co-workers arrived. Some purposefully came by to say hello and ask me how I was doing or how I was holding up…each greeted me with sad eyes.

Mid-way through the morning, I felt strong enough to dash out of my office for a bathroom break. More coworkers who I hadn't seen in a while asked me "how's the baby doing?" – those not knowing of Chloe's silent birth. I had to hold back tears, trying my best to explain what happened just 4 weeks ago. Some were shocked, others seemed to be understanding, and there were a few that just wanted to hug me. I embraced them, desperately needing those hugs, too.

A quick 4-minute trip turned into almost an hour. I made it back into the office, keeping my head down, trying to avoid as much eye contact as possible. As I began logging back into my workstation, another co-worker decided to come visit and ask me how I was doing. Immediately before he could speak, the energy shifted, and I just knew that this conversation was not going to be like the others.

There was no sadness in his eyes. If anything, he appeared to be inquisitive and forcing himself to say something.

While trying to maintain my professionalism and multi-task, he asked me, "Christina, how are you doing?"

I responded, "Okay, for a Monday. How about yourself?"

He promptly responds… "Good! Listen, I didn't want to take up too much of your time. I know that you are busy being off for a while and all. I did want to share with you my condolences."

"Thank you so much," I said, holding back tears.

He then responds, "At least you have your son."

I looked up. The water in my eyes quickly dried. It took so much in me not to react in pure anger. He then turned around, showing a weak smile, and walked away.

Immediately, I shut my door and broke.

May 3rd, 2008, my stillborn

Jemima Sadoella

After a few years, this particular day got less hard. But then, as I watched my rainbow child, my daughter, grow…the pain resurfaced. In 2008, I gave birth to a boy. He was born too soon, after a pregnancy of 20 weeks. I held him in my arms, hoping that, by some miracle, he would start to breathe on his own. He didn't, and a week later, we buried him.

Last year, in May, I cried on this day. The pain felt exactly like in the beginning. Three weeks after that day, I got pregnant again. This was 7 years after my rainbow child. I got blessed with a boy, just like my heart desired.

But people like to think that because you now have other children, you should get over losing your baby. Like having children after your loss will make up for it. My children are both unique and special on their own. They are NOT a replacement!

This year, it's tough again because my stillborn son would have been 12 years old. I can't help but wonder what he would've been like. Not having anybody who understands this, anybody to talk to or hold you, or just being there for you on a day like this…makes it even more painful. People just want you to let it go. They will never understand.

Mommies with a baby angel…stay strong…you are not alone. If you are going through this in your life, we should be there for each other. Women and mothers are always expected to be strong. We are never allowed to just have a moment. Well, let's just take that moment!

I know what it is like to feel like nobody understands you and you are alone. If you need to talk to somebody, don't be shy and just look around. More women than you might expect have suffered the same kind of loss and are hurting in silence as well.

Let's blow a kiss to the sky and always keep our angels in our hearts.

August Sunflower

Buki Hannaway

A sunflower grew in my garden
Shifted my forever twice over
With no apology or pardon
At first, I froze
Stuck in time
Consumed unable to process emotion
Unsure whether to soften or harden

A sunflower grew in my garden
Light beam cultivated to seed
I had prepared for an evergreen
Made space for what I thought this tree of life would need
Cleared out yesterdays
Danced for rain
Worshiped the sun
Salutations at dawn

A sunflower grew in my garden
My being honors that we are eternally one
This soul restless with questions
These arms know you are gone
No pattering feet
Just the memory of my favorite heartbeat
With every colour you've painted a new landscape
At times, an overwhelming kaleidoscope
I can't even explain how, but I cope

A sunflower grew in my garden
New soils combined with preloved grains gifted from our village
Collectively awaiting the beginning of a lifetime
Imagining a particular type of growth
Envisaging the sunshine you'd bring to mine
Removing the weeds that remained from all the cycle breaking
Long before your roots had sprouted

Or so I thought
A beautiful tragic surprise
Too brief a sunrise

A sunflower grew in my garden
You are not the foliage I expected
Shining sun rays on the wounds I neglected
You are the story ancestors divine curated
When I feel comfort from traveling breeze
Endless pains begin to ease
A reminder that, like you, I am luminary
With every part of me, I wish those moments
Were beyond momentary
But I smile, knowing a life so brief, is the most legendary

Cacao Tree Still Births

Camari Carter Hawkins

Tour guide tells me the cacao tree is most fruitful 35 years, lives until 80.
He repeats this fact more than any others, then says, it's much like life.
Was that message for me, a probe in my anxiety and my pending womb,
motherless frame with angels for children?
I want to believe that I will, too, birth cacao fruits with seeds of their own.

My body still has your name on it.
                    —DéJunae "Day-Juh-D" Johnson

He Knows

Déjunae "Day-Juh-D" Johnson

My body still has your name on it
Even though I never named you
I'm feeling kind of weighed from it
Even though I've barely carried you
Your brother is calling out for you
Even though I never spoke of you…to him

He knows
My soul knows
My body knows
Why would I let my mind forget if…
He knows
My soul knows
My body knows

Remembering Peach

Lauren (crunchymamadfw)

It has been almost two years since my miscarriage. I can't help but reflect on that day. I have never really shared exactly what happened the day that we found out about our loss. People often don't ask too many questions when talking about this type of loss because they want to show empathy and not be intrusive. I completely understand that, but I also think that it's important to talk about what happened. 1 in 4 women will experience pregnancy and or infant loss. It happens more often than we think—it happened to me. I am 1 in 4, and this is my story.

My husband and I decided that we would start trying for a baby late in the Summer of 2015. It took two cycles for us to conceive, and we couldn't have been happier. We were ecstatic. My first appointment with the OBGYN was at about 5 weeks. I was very early, but at that appointment, we saw our baby. It all became so incredibly real. There was actual life growing inside of me.

The next week, we had another appointment, and we saw our baby's heartbeat flashing rhythmically on the sonogram screen. It was the most beautiful thing I'd ever seen. A little over a week after that, we had another appointment. I was almost 8 weeks.

That appointment began like any other—uneventful. We sat in the waiting room. Smiled at the other mamas and mamas-to-be. They finally called my name. I was so excited to see my little Peach again. The sonogram tech greeted us with a smile and began by squirting the warm gel on my belly. She rubbed the wand on my stomach and looked at the screen. We exchanged small talk, and then she went cold as ice and stopped talking. She looked at the screen carefully and moved the wand more. First on the left side of my belly, then to the right. She went silent. So silent I couldn't even hear her breathe. I looked her in the eyes for reassurance. I wanted her to tell us that everything was okay. Her eyes refused to meet mine. At that moment, I knew. I knew something was wrong. She got up suddenly and turned off the monitor. She said that the doctor would be in shortly.

She left the room, and my husband and I sank in the silence of that room, knowing that something had gone terribly wrong. Unable to control it any longer, I laid there quietly sobbing.

Finally, a nurse came in and guided us to a private room. On the way to the room, I saw the sonogram tech sitting solemnly in the hallway, still refusing to look at me. We got to the room, and the doctor came in shortly after. He walked in and instantly put his hand on my shoulder and said, "I'm sorry." I can still feel how heavy his hand felt on my shoulder. I knew it was coming, but that didn't lessen the pain. It felt as if I'd been hit by a truck. I couldn't breathe, I couldn't see, I couldn't think. I sat in that room crying uncontrollably in my husband's arms while his own tears dropped on my shoulder.

The doctor scheduled a D&C a few days later on November 13th, it was a Friday. My nurse came in to have me fill out and sign the necessary paperwork. Before she could finish, she burst into tears and had to leave the room. I remember thinking that this was the saddest moment in my entire life. I didn't think I'd ever pick up the pieces.
A couple weeks after the D&C, we got paperwork in the mail that told us why our baby had died. Triploidy. This meant that she had an extra set of chromosomes. This condition almost always results in a miscarriage. Even if the pregnancy goes to term, babies born with triploidy rarely survive.

Grief was extremely hard, and it came in overwhelming waves that drowned me. It really did. My bad days were really bad, and even on my "good" days, I'd feel guilty for having the audacity to smile. Working through that grief was a process. f it wasn't for my husband, family, and getting to the point where I was no longer angry at God, I don't know if I ever would have gotten out of that dark place.

Yes, some time has passed, but it's still not easy accepting that one day, there was life growing in my womb, and the next day that precious little life was no longer. I still think about her often. I wonder what she would have been like and what she would have looked like, but I am at peace, and that's all I can ask for.

Pregnancy Test

Camari Carter Hawkins

I keep it.
The positive pregnancy test
It's the last sign I have that confirms
I was a mother
Am a mother

Settled like coffin at my bedside
I can't get rid of

I can bottle up the blood river on the floor
Bury in mason jar
it'll grow
green, fuzzy
I still name it,
my baby

And when the growth takes over
Becomes black
It is my child's skin
and hope
for a heartbeat

And when baby seeps through the lid
I'll plant it in the backyard
to grow a willow tree
where I will sit under my baby

Birthing Vision: When Pain Led to Pressure and Pressure Created Promise

Sabrina Tindal Cherry

There he was in my arms. He looked so perfect and so peaceful. His tiny little hands. His feet. Even his eyelashes had begun to form. Our perfect son. I could not have asked for a more gracious blessing—the gift of being with him in that moment. To see his face.

Lewis and I were like any other eager set of parents: over-excited and excessively cautious. It was our first pregnancy and we wanted to take extra care in every way imaginable. We carefully noted when we had doctor's appointments, making sure not to miss any. Initial pregnancy test and confirmation. Check. First ultrasound. Check. And specialty visits to my endocrinologist. Check.

As the months passed, my body changed in ways I don't recall ever hearing or reading about. And it all seemed to be happening so swiftly. Since I was employed at a hospital, I took advantage of the ability to wear scrubs to work, adding an extra layer of comfort and ease to my growing belly and body.

We made it! We were at the medically designated, safe 12-week period. Up until that time, we hadn't told anyone about our precious, little secret: we had a growing peanut. With Thanksgiving just around the corner, we knew our parents would be the first to receive the news. We hosted them at our home and managed to hide my little bump for the entire weekend. Finally, on their last day of the holiday visit, we asked them to sit down. With faces as serious as we could muster, we shared with them that we had some news. The look of dismay on their faces let us know they were worried. Had something happened? Were we getting divorced?

We didn't leave them in suspense for too long—that seemed a bit cruel. We spilled the beans. We're pregnant! As my mother's only child, I knew she would be through the roof excited. She was. Joy and elation filled her face as she first scorned me for making her nervous and then squeezed me tight with excitement. Lewis's family was no less thrilled. We celebrated and rejoiced together, answering their flurry of questions. When did you find out? When is the baby due? Do you know the gender? So many questions. So much happiness and so very much excitement.

The weeks rushed by and before we knew it the Christmas season was upon us. We decided to travel to Asheville for the holiday and took our first baby bump photo with me sitting in an oversized sleigh in front of an equally oversized fireplace at the Grove Park Inn. I knew my belly was growing but I didn't realize just how much until I saw our pictures from the mini getaway. Perhaps more than before, it hit me that I was carrying an entire little human being.

In January, we traveled to central Illinois to celebrate with another family member who was also having a baby. We'd carefully selected our gift, wanting to plant a small seed in this young couple's life as they ventured into parenthood. We'd also selected that weekend as the time to share our pregnancy news with the remainder of Lewis's family.

Although no one said anything, many of them gasped in relief at the little weight I'd put on—now aware that it was because of our growing peanut and not overindulgence in all things yummy. Again, we celebrated, laughed, cried, and rejoiced.

The weekend was a whirlwind and we were back at the airport headed home. I needed one last pit stop to the restroom as this minor inconvenience seemed to be ever-increasing. As I sat down to relieve myself, I felt an unfamiliar goosh of liquid. When I saw the small puddle of water on the floor I knew something had happened. Something terrible had happened. I immediately grabbed my phone with tears beginning to crowd my eyes and hands trembling as I called for Lewis to come to the restroom.

My water had broken prematurely. The doctors were unable to pinpoint why this happened but talked us through the possibilities for the near future, as well as if we were able to make it to full term. We decided we would return home after a safe release from the hospital so we could speak with our primary care team.

After a few more days in the hospital and one nervous plane ride, we were back at home and headed for an immediate visit to my OB. The medical team was concerned about how our peanut would survive with such little amniotic fluid. We were presented with a range of options, including terminating the pregnancy. But we decided that if our peanut had hung in there, so would we. I was put on bedrest with very strict guidelines related to work, household activity, and driving. I was grateful for a job that allowed me to take however much time I needed to heal and have a healthy remainder of my pregnancy.

The days quickly grew lonely. Although Lewis and I spent time together when he was home from work, the times he was away felt extremely isolating. I dove into televangelists and reading just to find inspiration for every single moment…to keep my mind from wandering about all the horrible things that could happen. One of my sorority sisters and friends knew how much I love to read and mailed me a box of books to help in my productive, but limited activity. A few people from my church stopped by to sit with me and pray for me. In spite of the loneliness, I felt surrounded by love, hope, and encouragement.

But there is also something about that level and intensity of silence that begets introspection. I wanted our child to live. I wanted to be a great wife. I wanted to have a healthy family, but what had I sacrificed in the pursuit of these things? What happened to my dreams of returning to school? Or engaging in more meaningful work? What about my dreams of writing books? Or starting a scholarship for young women from my hometown? Over the next few weeks, I felt convicted. I'd become so singular-focused on my pursuit of marriage and family that I snuffed out every other dream I had.

While my heart continued racing as I reflected on the dreams I'd let go of, so did my mind. I spent a lot of days in angst. Any spot of blood or hint of pain sent me into a panic. My days seemed to be filled with isolation, introspection, and angst. But we held on. I kept praying and began to believe that if our son had made it this far, we would be okay. We just needed a few more weeks and I would be admitted to the hospital to have my labor induced. We could do it. We would do it!

On a day that seemed like any other, I started experiencing light cramping. I spoke with the on-call doctor and was instructed to begin timing the increments between when I felt pain. The pain continued, but not in what was deemed alarming in any way. We were now late into the evening and I was advised to take some Tylenol to help me get a bit of rest and to call back immediately if anything changed. I followed the doctor's orders and fell asleep for a short period of time. I was exhausted, in every way. I was mentally exhausted from the weeks of worry. I was physically exhausted from—ironically—doing little to nothing. I wanted a little rest. I needed to rest.

Around 4 a.m., I woke up to go to the restroom. Great! Not only was I tired, but now I was constipated in the wee hours of the morning. But then I felt something so strange, so awkward—I knew…again, something had happened.

Just like that, our son—Carter Alexander Cherry—arrived. Through both Lewis's and my cries of despair, we could barely hear the instructions from the 911 operator. But she persisted, guiding us through every carefully detailed step, reminding us to breathe, and assuring us someone would be with us swiftly. Lewis was so amazing! He displayed such courage and strength on that morning as we did the unimaginable while waiting for EMS.

Our ride to the hospital was the longest ever. And the next few days were no less manageable. My time in the hospital was filled with visits from Chaplins, a host of medical professionals, and Lewis. Even as my mind felt foggy and my heart felt empty, I was still grateful. I knew our moment of tragedy could have been so much worse had I been home alone. I was grateful for prompt emergency care and effective follow-up treatments to ensure my physical body could begin recovering. I was grateful for the Chaplins, for their prayers, and for their care during our time of loss.

I returned home and my mom came to stay with us for a few days. Just having her close made me feel even more comforted. Lewis and I took a short trip to the mountains just to get away from it all, to have some time to reconnect, and to be in a place of solitude with one another.

Following my release from the hospital, I had another three weeks of medical leave. But I also had a renewed sense of life and purpose. Losing Carter was and remains one of the most devastating losses of my life. During my time on bed rest and after his transition, I knew that event would and could kill me…emotionally, spiritually, mentally, and ultimately, physically. I knew the difficulty of being resilient after experiencing such crippling trauma. I knew I had to search for some sort of purpose in the pain.

We attended a few infant loss groups for couples but the stories were hard. As we were carrying our own grief, it became unbearable to hear and carry the grief of others—many stories much more devastating than ours. We resorted to couples counseling with a grief therapist. As she worked with us on processing our loss, I opened my heart to seeking new meaning in my life.

Seven months after our loss, I started school at Candler School of Theology in Atlanta, Georgia. Five years later I graduated from the University of Georgia with my doctorate degree in Public Health and began my dream job as a college professor just a few months later. Unfortunately, during this period Lewis and I also divorced, but today I find meaning in other ways. Each day I get to teach, write, and speak with intention as I continue to see ways God uses our most debilitating moments to birth purpose and promise.

Our journey was not easy and I firmly believe that my story is still being told. I am still learning all the ways I believe God is using that painful moment in my life to bless other women; to help me face challenging times with hope and expectation; and to remain open to my life being recreated in unimaginable ways. Here are just a few things that have continued to help me.

1. It was imperative that Lewis and I took time to heal. As endearing as all the phone calls, text messages, and gifts were, we needed a moment. I needed a moment to gather my thoughts, to sit in deep and meaningful ways with my grief, and to settle my heart. **Take the time you need.** This doesn't mean unhealthy isolation, but it does mean giving yourself time to begin the healing process before feeling obligated to answer anyone's questions or allow them to take up space in your life.

2. Once I began interacting with others, aside from my immediate family and close friends, I was very intentional about how I re-engaged. I sent an email to my colleagues before returning to work, letting them know what conversations and questions were off-limits. There were some people I talked with right away and others I didn't re-engage with for months because I knew they lacked respect for the boundaries I needed. Although we don't often have as much control in curating our interactions in this way, I knew I could proactively express my needs in a few places. This made a significant difference. **Be intentional about re-engaging in meaningful community**.

3. For some couples, putting the loss behind them is their approach to moving on and exploring new options—including trying to conceive again. For me, I wanted to honor Carter. I wanted to remember him and have our time together as a centering part of my life. The summer after our loss, I created *Carter's Blog Corner* as a way to pick up an art I'd treasured since childhood and abandoned in adulthood. I've consistently blogged on *Carter's Corner* for eleven years. My ex-husband has done other things to honor our son. In our own ways, we've intentionally communicated time and time again, "We will not forget you. Your life mattered and still matters." **Find ways to honor your loss.**

4. On many occasions, I have discussed the weight of grief. Although no loss is easy, when my grandfather died it felt different. When other family members with debilitating illnesses transitioned, it also felt different. Losing a child is so unexpected and losing a child the way I did—when and how I delivered—is nothing short of traumatic. The grief felt unbearable. I believe my time at home on bed rest and the clarity of vision for my life's next steps were my saving grace. As hard as it can be, I encourage you to **think about how your loss can help you to rebirth new possibilities**. Perhaps, this is remaining committed to trying to conceive again after your body has healed. *And* there may be other dreams you let die. Is there a place you want to volunteer? Is there a ministry you've procrastinated on starting? Is there a trip you want to take? An apology or reconciliation you want to extend? It may take some time—years even—but I do believe the pain can create meaningful pressure to reconsider life after loss.

5. Grief is long. Grief is spontaneous. Grief is a process. **Grief is a journey.** I had to accept that there wasn't a finite time when my grief would end. Instead, it has evolved. It definitely doesn't hurt as much, but there are moments when I think of Carter, and my heart is saddened. There are times when I see photos of families or hear stories about Mother's Day and I have to acknowledge the emptiness in my heart. I've learned to honor these moments and my process. I try to be intentional about holidays, especially Mother's Day, and find ways to celebrate other blessings such as the joy of still being able to spend time with my mom. I've also joined in celebrating with others. Many of my friends who also experienced miscarriages and stillbirths now have healthy babies. I celebrate with them! This has helped heal my heart.

6. I've mentioned this before, but I can't stress how important it is to **reimagine life.** In my late 20s and early 30s, I had a vision of marriage and children, and onward from there. In my 40s I have a very different life, but it is a life I would not trade for anything else. Daily, I get to surrender my plans, my dreams, and my visions in exchange for something greater. I want to invite you to reimagine your life and all the ways it can be fulfilling, as well as meaningful, even if it doesn't look exactly as you thought it would.

7. When I let go of life as I thought I would have been and embraced what was unfolding, the unexpected happened! Doors and windows opened! I traveled to places I never dreamed of and gained access to opportunities I never imagined. On a regular basis, I look at my life in awe. It is not what I thought it would be, nor is it perfect but it is greater than I ever imagined. And this greatness is not exclusive to my enjoyment. I believe I now live an intentional life focused on significance to and for others. I get to live a life that routinely asks, "How can I serve someone today? What can I do to make a positive difference in the life of someone else?" **Be open to the unexpected happening in your life!**

Our loss was eleven years ago. Not a day goes by that I don't think about how really hard moments can push us toward new dreams, enabling us to birth new purposes. For many families, this means trying to conceive again and perhaps, exploring alternative means of becoming a parent. But there are also those of us who will not go on to have a healthy pregnancy. We must tell the stories of women who were unable to conceive for whatever reason, but decided to foster or adopt. There are those of us who faced double losses through miscarriages (or stillborns) and marriages. We must tell the stories of women who felt societal pressures to pursue marriage and motherhood, even when these dreams may not have aligned with their most intimate desires. We almost must tell the stories of women who wanted these things, who felt the crippling effect of these dreams slipping through their hands, and who went on to live fulfilling lives despite this. These stories need to be told. Our stories need to be told. Women need to know there are many ways to birth vision, promise, and joy into the world. No, none of these compare to motherhood or sharing our lives with loving partners, but we can still birth significance and meaning. We must tell these stories. These stories matter. My story matters. Your story matters.

Numb

Quianna Ford

Each time more painful Imagining your faces
as you slip away.
My heart's only desire
To be your mother
I will never let it go
But loss becomes home
And daybreak arrives, hopeless
For faded heartbeats.

My invisible loss was palpable to me...
—JoAnna Pendergrass, DVM

Where does the pain go when it goes away?

Camari Carter Hawkins

When the avocado pit in my soul allows itself to be scooped out
and I am left a hallow, healed body
face up in tender prayer
I believe there is a pain angel
who wears a green apron that carries that pit,
buries it
along other sorrowfuls like willow and cedar
in time
that pit becomes tree
yielding a careful fruit
to eat and learn from

Grief

JoAnna Pendergrass, DVM

I didn't really know what grief was until I had my first miscarriage in December 2018, when I was about 7 weeks pregnant. Nothing prepares you for losing an unborn child. There's no guidebook for how to grieve an invisible loss.

In an 11-day whirlwind that December, I found out that I was pregnant, found out that I miscarried, and had a dilation & curettage procedure to surgically remove the pregnancy tissue from my uterus. To say that the rug was cruelly pulled out from under me is an understatement.

Until that miscarriage, I had only a vague understanding of the stages of grief. Our marriage therapist told me that I just had to walk through the grieving process. I had to experience grief for myself and then come out on the other side.

Fortunately, it didn't take me long to accept my miscarriage, as bewildering as it was. I didn't blame myself or my husband. I didn't torture myself with "What if" questions.

But accepting my miscarriage didn't stop the emotional roller coaster. Nor did it shield me from feeling empty when seeing a pregnant woman or a baby in a stroller. Rather, acceptance allowed me to give myself grace and not be too hard on myself about the miscarriage.

My invisible loss was palpable to me. The emptiness in my womb was painfully real. The emptiness would rise up unexpectedly. I would grip my stomach, the memories would come rushing back, and the tears would flow.

As I processed the loss with the help of my maternal mental health therapist, I learned that grief looks different for everyone and has no timeline.

After my first miscarriage, my grief ebbed and flowed. Most moments of most days, I was fine. In fact, I would have stretches of days when I didn't think about my miscarriage at all. But, any number of early mornings, my mind would relive the miscarriage, and the feelings of emptiness and loss would completely overwhelm me.

Trying to talk about intimacy would inevitably leave me in tears or choked up, my grief leaving me unable to speak; in my mind, intimacy and loss were now inextricably tied. One evening, shortly after the D&C, simply folding the shirt I'd worn to the hospital stirred up intense grief.

Balancing my grief with the hope of getting pregnant again was tricky. In the several months of trying to get pregnant for a second time, my grief would intensify every time I got my period. Every period, every day of my period, was a reminder of the loss, a reminder that I wasn't pregnant.

My second pregnancy gave me a brief respite from actively grieving. The grief came back, though, when the second pregnancy also ended in miscarriage when I was just shy of being 10 weeks pregnant.

This second time around, grief wasn't new. It was familiar…but different. I didn't have the emotional rollercoasters. Moments of intense feelings of loss were rare. I even cried less. But the loss was still very, very real.

After my second miscarriage, I felt like I needed some type of tangible item to honor my two unborn children. I decided to get two brooches. Wearing them gave me a feeling of peace, a feeling that I would be okay.

With that second loss, I told my husband that I did not want to try to conceive again naturally. He supported me in that decision. We had a consultation appointment at our hospital's reproductive center and were told that IVF with pre-implantation genetic screening would be our best chance of becoming pregnant again and minimizing the risk of miscarriage.

Going through IVF was so consuming that there really wasn't much mental space left for grieving. It's not that I was 'over' my losses. It was that IVF became #1 in my mind and didn't leave room for much else. Then, grief manifested itself for a third time. My first round of IVF, in December 2019, failed because my eggs were immature and, therefore could not be fertilized. A third loss. A third lost chance of having a baby.

This third round of grief was different yet again. I actively fought against grieving. It was Christmas time, and I just didn't want to feel sad. I'd seen posts on Facebook and Instagram about how the holidays can be hard when you've experienced a loss, but I didn't pay them much attention.

Then, on Christmas Eve, it hit me. As I prepared to go out for a morning walk, all three losses came to the forefront of my mind. I remember telling my husband that I now realized why the holidays can be so hard. And yet, as I said the words, I swallowed back tears that were threatening to start flowing.

Once I let my guard down and finally allowed myself to feel the feelings that I'd pushed back about the failed IVF cycle, I was able to truly grieve and process that loss.

After that first cycle, I went through another two rounds of IVF. My husband and I were elated that, after all of the injections, monitoring appointments, and egg retrievals, we had four healthy embryos. In November 2020, I had my embryo transfer and became pregnant with my son, giving birth in July 2021.

Motherhood after infertility is a unique experience. I love my son and feel incredibly blessed to be a mother, yet still have moments of grief from my miscarriages.

Memories of my losses are not far below the surface. The emotional scars of miscarriage are still there. But I give myself grace and make room for experiencing the joys of motherhood while also mourning my losses. Joy and grief can exist simultaneously.

Overall, walking through the experience of grief taught me several lessons:

- *It's okay to not be okay.* Grief is normal after a miscarriage. Whatever feelings you have after having a miscarriage, experience them fully. Give yourself grace to not feel okay; it's all part of the process.
- *Just let it happen.* Before my miscarriages, I associated crying with weakness. Not anymore. When I feel tears come on, I tell myself, just let it happen. Let the tears flow. Crying is cathartic. After the tears stop, you can press the 'reset' button and keep moving forward.
- *Find peace in your grief.* Grief is painful and necessary. When you allow yourself to fully grieve, and just get everything out, you leave room within that grief to eventually make peace with your loss.

There are still days when I question why God made these two miscarriages part of my life story. Part of me wishes that they'd never happened. Yet, had they not happened, I wouldn't have learned how to grieve. And, I wouldn't have experienced the peace and ultimate joy of making it to the other side of grief.

The babies look at me as if they know

Camari Carter Hawkins

As if my baby told them
if you see my mommy
tell her I'm alright
These babies at the store, park, DMV line
have been looking for me
an amber alert blares for me
Their faces flash railroad signals
as I cross their path
Their gummy cheeks spread open.
They reach for me
to tell me something

I wish I knew how to talk to these angels
I watch their hands
move in circular motion
then close together.
I watch them again and again
always the same
hands, gestures.
They saw my baby on their way here

I will tell these babies to deliver a message
Tell my baby,
I am here
I am okay
        but not okay.

And we wait...

—Jina Ward

Thoughts in Waiting

Estee Marie

I feared once life would begin prematurely
Ironically following, I feared life wouldn't begin at all
Now I wonder if it's worth it
       to watch a miracle develop over the course of time…

The Wait

Jina Ward

Being a Mother was all I ever wanted. I do not remember having another ambition. I had this whole plan of meeting the perfect man, getting married and having my 2.5 kids with the white picket-fenced house. I wanted the whole saccharine fairytale. I met my husband in college. It was love at first sight and we fell hard really fast. I dropped out of school soon after we met because I really did not want to be there anyway. What did it matter? We would be married soon and my career would be being a wife and raising our children.

While dating my husband we would experience a miscarriage. Having a child before marriage was not in my original plan. I arrogantly thought, with some slight modifications I could still have my plan. We would just get married while I was pregnant, and continue on with our perfect life. Imagine my shock and dismay when I miscarried. I was angry. How could this be? My plan was totally dismantled. We were now going to wait to get married and we did not have a child. I was angry for a whole year. So mad that I do not even remember that year. It was a dark time of me being inconsolable and swimming in a pool of negativity.

Our wait had begun…

We would get married two years later. Right away we started trying. We were not getting pregnant, and I was becoming increasingly depressed. With the help of the psychologist, I discovered one of the reasons I was depressed was that I had not made a decision about what to do with my life while I was waiting to have a child. I was feeling stagnant because it was as if I was putting my life on hold. I started a period of discovering myself. I figured out I liked to read, liked fashion and became a foodie. I went back to school to become an interior designer.

Three years into marriage we started infertility treatments. The first procedure we did was an IUI. I had my scarred down fallopian tube removed and then immediately started meds to stimulate my ovaries. I was sensitive to the meds physically and they made me moody. I was also completely overwhelmed. I was in school at the time and my husband was newly in his career. Nine years together and we still did not really know each other that well. We still argued quite a bit. We had not figured out how to leverage our opposing strengths and weaknesses to be a better unit. We were young and broke and had accomplished much in our careers or traveled. After the IUI the doctor told us to have more intercourse to increase our chances. My husband set his alarm so we could do the deed before work. When his alarm sounded, he turned it off and we woke up late. I was enraged! All I could think about was how my body was going through a lot of changes, physically, emotionally and mentally and all he had to do was remember to have sex with me. I was so resentful and angry. I felt like the weight of infertility rested on my shoulders. We were not ready to embark on this pandora's box of decisions, issues and emotions that come with infertility journeys. Most obviously we were not ready to adapt our life.

We decided to wait ten years.

During the ten years, I finished my Interior Design degree and my husband became more comfortable in his career. I worked in interior design for three years and then started a career in travel. I had amazing travel perks, so we traveled all over the world. In our travels, we enjoyed local culture, explored out of our comfort zone, and had many unique and wonderful experiences. We threw lavish parties with our friends. We ate fantastic food. We went to the most amazing places. We had the best time, just the two of us living our best life. It was a time when we did any and everything we wanted to do. Many times, on a whim's notice. We really embraced and celebrated our time with no children. We still wanted a child, but the infertility journey was on the back burner.

When I was 34, my Mom asked me if I wanted to still have a child. We found an infertility doctor, and the process started again. My remaining fallopian tube was scarred down so much dye could barely pass through. It was determined that IVF would be the best route. Funny thing is, I wanted to adopt if I could not have a child without treatment. However, my husband wanted to try. He had never asked anything of me. I wanted to honor his request. I knew intuitively we were in for the fight of our lives. Immediately, we came up with an action plan. The plan started with me asking for help so that I would not be resentful of the demands IVF was placing on me. My husband agreed to uphold doing whatever I needed him to do. There would be no resentment because we would work as a team. We would give each other grace and leeway for imperfections.

The retrieval went well. We had seven great-quality embryos. The first transfer went well. I got pregnant with twins. We miscarried at 13 weeks. We were devastated. We thought this was it. My husband asked, "Why us?" I remember thinking at that moment, "Why not us?" It was the beginning of a perspective shift. I started thinking about how arrogant it was to think we deserved this child just because we thought we had checked all the right boxes and had done everything right. Did we think we were above hardships, and that they just happened to other people? I began to realize we needed to have the mindset of having all the hope but no expectations.

With the next transfer, I got pregnant, and my water broke at 15 weeks. A doctor on call asked us to abort immediately because the odds were stacked against our daughter living. I had a choice to make. I could take the easy way out or fight. I choose to fight. I carried our daughter for 8 weeks. Because I had learned to give up expectations, while being on bedrest, I became totally present. I allowed myself to feel all of the emotions, but I did not allow myself to stay in them. This was in stark contrast to my response after miscarrying so many years ago. As a person that prided themselves on never asking anybody for anything, I learned to lean on my amazing support village. By doing that a lot of my relationships strengthen. I spent my time encouraging women in online groups experiencing the same thing I was going through to get my mind off myself. I became extremely grateful for everything. Our daughter lived only 12 hours. No one wants to lose their child. The pain of it never fully goes away. What does happen is it becomes less raw as time goes on. I learned to focus on the good. I am extremely grateful we got to meet her. I also rest well with no regrets because we did our very best for her. What started off scary and uncertain, ended up being my greatest lesson in resilience and where I learned to be a WARRIOR.

We would then go on to experience two missed adoptions. The first missed adoption was the hardest. In some ways, it was harder than losing my own daughter. When my water broke, we knew we might not have our daughter, and I had 8 weeks to reconcile that. With the adoption, I held that baby. We made all the plans in our life and home for that baby. It was supposed to be a sure thing. We were so close to being parents. It felt like the rug had been pulled away from us. I started to go into the woe is me, but I did not allow myself to stay there. The 2nd adoption was not quite as hard because we figured out right away that the mother was trying to extort money from us. That one just made me angry. Both fueled my decision to carry on with our remaining embryos.

I was the only person who wanted to proceed with the final embryos. Everyone, including my husband, did not want me to experience any further pain. I just had to finish it out. Once the decision was made, he was 100% committed. Everyone else's opinion did not matter. We came up with a blueprint of what we would do if we did not have a child. The blueprint included travel, buying a new house, and career changes. The plan gave us something to look forward to, so we did not become hyper-focused on the outcome. We had three embryos that were supposed to be two more tries. When they went to defrost, one of the embryos did not do well. So, this would be our final chance to have a baby through IVF. Instead of panicking, we trusted the process and went forward. We implanted, and I got pregnant. We faced many challenges in this pregnancy. But the whole time, I was calm. I held fast to my philosophy of what will be will be. I was able to stay present and enjoy much of the pregnancy. The pregnancy ended in success and my son was born healthy and beautiful. I was 42 when he was born. It was one of the best moments of my life.

Our entire infertility journey was 22 years.

The wait was disappointing, frustrating, depressing, eye-opening, fun and challenging.

It was all of this and so much more. Most importantly, it was a training ground that highlighted my unique character and my resilience. The evolution of how dark and hopeless my life was after the first miscarriage to how strong I was after losing my child is truly remarkable. I am so proud of myself for choosing to be fully present and not put my life on hold while waiting. I learned I could do the hard things and live through and thrive!

Blessing Day, Every February 8th

Camari Carter Hawkins

Cloudy eyes shed for you
Willow womb weeps for you

A four year tree you'd be today
All opinioned and independent
I'll never know the fruit you'd become
or help you peel back layers to reveal
your seeded gifts

Hundreds of birds sang to me today
while I walked
I imagine them you
Singing me it's okay
you'll be okay

It is the wonder
The never knowing
The hope I get to one days
I can't seem to get over
Until Heaven meets earth
I'm grateful I once had you
I'll see you again

It's the Wards

Trulawnia Ward

In 2010, I started seeing my gynecologist regularly. We went over my history, and she questioned my "issues." I knew my "issues" weren't normal, but I didn't know they could be so problematic or could potentially wreak havoc on my body. She asked me if I wanted to have kids. When I said yes, she proceeded to run bloodwork. At my follow-up appointment, she told me I had hyperprolactinemia, or abnormally high levels of the hormone prolactin in my blood, and I would need to see a specialist.

When I saw him, he said, "Well, it's high, but I don't know why she sent you to me because it's not extremely high."

I then had an MRI because this condition was also indicative of a pituitary tumor. Sure enough, there it was. It was micro, though, so there was no need for surgery at the moment.

When I went back to the gynecologist, she let me know that it would be difficult for me to have children IF I was able to have them at all. I've always wanted a big family, and early, but it was then that I knew I was against the clock. By this time, I was engaged, so I knew I needed to be ready after the wedding.

But let's pause right there—this is the part where everyone starts to ask questions and give unsolicited advice.

"Why did you wanna get married so young?"

"Didn't you want to live your life?"

"You're getting MARRIED??!"

"Take your time. You're still young..."

And the one that hurt me the most:

"Wait to have kids. You don't need to jump into marriage and start having kids."

That last statement may as well have been a knife that slit my throat. It was at that very moment I knew I wouldn't be able to count on certain people for support. And I got it. People try to give advice and mean well. But you never know what a person is going through. So every move I made after that, I kept to myself.

Year after year, I received the same results from the MRIs and blood tests over and over again. I finally decided to switch doctors because we were getting NOWHERE! And so the search for a new doctor began.

By 2013 I found a new doctor. In between the last one and this new one, I researched what I needed and wanted for my treatment. When I got to my first appointment, after doing her thing, the doctor sat me down and asked me what I wanted to do. In order to receive fertility assistance, you have to have been Trying To Conceive (or TTC) for at least a year. I told her I wanted the infertility treatment, Clomid. She okayed it, and wrote me the prescription. I completed six months of treatment, the maximum amount of rounds, and still NOTHING!

She briefly went over the possibility of Polycystic Ovary Syndrome (PCOS) because she believed I was borderline, and then referred me to a Reproductive Endocrinologist. Another specialist, yay!

When I saw him in 2014, he confirmed my PCOS diagnosis and switched my prescription to Femara (aka Letrozole), which decreases the amount of estrogen in the body.

After multiple months of trying while on Femara and 2+ years of trying in total, the treatment finally worked! Two years is maybe not the longest time to struggle, but it was a battle for me, especially mentally. I was doing this ALONE.

I graduated from seeing the Reproductive Endocrinologist after about two months of being pregnant and returned to my regular obstetrician. Everything was going well until I reached 20 weeks.

I started to feel like I was peeing on myself. I thought maybe I had a weak bladder. This went on for about a week and it started to get worse. When I mentioned it to my mom, she encouraged me to see a doctor, so we went together to the hospital late one night. After being checked out, it was determined to be amniotic fluid. I stayed at the hospital, and the next day my doctor told me the plan of care. They had to do a scan, and it revealed the baby barely had a pocket of fluid. She diagnosed me with oligohydramnios, a disorder affecting amniotic fluid.

She decided to admit me at 22 weeks and I would have to stay there until 34 weeks when she would induce me– IF I made it that far. I could not get out of bed. I could not leave my room. I had to use a bedpan if I had use the bathroom. Extreme, I know. I argued that I would lose more fluid trying to get on a bedpan than just using a bedside pot At first she refused, but my nurses asked again, and she agreed. So, I could finally step out of my bed.

I saw my doctor every day, but for only MAYBE two minutes before she was out. A few times, she made slick remarks that would have gotten her told off if I wasn't half asleep. A couple of the other doctors would drop by and talk to me or maybe watch videos or whatever we were watching (we had literally moved into the hospital). Meanwhile, my own doctor had no time for me!

I was trapped in my room for weeks and weeks, and then my senses started to go off. Something was about to happen, but I didn't know what. I asked my doctor if she could deliver my baby if I wanted her to, and she said no, which is understandable to an extent. I was only at about 26 weeks, and I had developed a few infections, which I caught and mentioned to my nurses. The last one I got, my doctor just so happened to be in the room, and so I told her. She asked me what I was feeling and when I told her, she blatantly said, "I'm not going to test you because you don't have the typical symptoms." FIRST OF ALL, EXCUSE

ME?! I NEVER have the "typical symptoms," and you already know I have a history of this!

Days went by, and I started having tissue-y discharge. Strange. I collected it and showed my nurse, and she had never seen anything like it before and didn't know what it was. She showed the other nurses, and NO ONE knew what it was. They didn't dismiss me, though. They told me to show the doctor the next day and said she would likely send it to the pathology lab. When I showed my obstetrician the next day, she looked at it and said, "I'm not sure what this is. I would normally send this to the pathology lab, but I'm not gonna send it."

WTF!?!???

By this time, I had been in the hospital for nearly two months, and I was stir-crazy. I had only been out of my room when I went upstairs for an ultrasound to check on the baby two or three times and when my nurse wheeled me around the halls and outside twice with an ON CALL doctor! Not even my own doctor! Shame on my doctor, huh?! Yeah, I know! PITIFUL! 7 WEEKS!

On March 8, at 29 weeks, my cervical mucus plug came out, which indicates labor is right around the corner. I was checked out by an on-call doctor who said I was still only two centimeters dilated, but because I had never been dilated before that, I knew I was in labor. When I woke up the next morning, Jason was born at 2lbs 7oz.

The doctors showed him to me and brought him to the side. A nurse leaned over and said, "You went into labor because you have an infection!" And it all came together!

They brought him out to the waiting room to let the family quickly see him, and then rushed him off to the NICU. Everything went downhill from there.

The doctors finished up with me, and, for a moment, I thought I was good, but then I couldn't stop shaking. I was taken to the postpartum floors and still couldn't stop shaking. My family was there, and they each took turns going to see the baby, but I hadn't yet. I felt so weak, and no one said anything to me about my care. I was in and out of consciousness, shivering and whatnot, trying to stay awake for company.

NICU doctors came and told me they might have to do a blood transfusion. I signed the paperwork, and they were gone. I was in and out of consciousness, shivering and whatnot, trying to stay awake for company.

Around 10 that night, after my family had left, the NICU doctors came back and gave us the news: our baby would likely not make it, and we should go down to the NICU right away. I had no updates other than the paperwork they had me sign earlier that day, so I was shocked. When we got to the NICU, we held him, and he left us in our arms.

I'm in utter disbelief when I get back to the room, and now had to somehow stomach the pain of calling my family and telling them what had happened. I had been numb for years already, so I couldn't even cry because the whole journey just felt so unreal. I had not even caught up to reality yet.

When our family and friends got back to the hospital, they took turns holding him. As I held him and looked at him, the anger began to pour in, but still, I had no tears. If I crashed, who would have picked me up?! I had to keep myself together for everyone else, but I was more angry than anything else.

That night was one of my worst nights ever. I had a fever, was shivering, and soaked my clothes and bed sheets with sweat. I had to change my clothes multiple times overnight. Nurses constantly checked my blood pressure because it was bottoming out. Fever...all the sorts.

The next day, the doctor didn't come to check on me. The nurse on the floor came and told me I was septic. So, that's what was happening to me! I couldn't leave until the sepsis was under control with antibiotics. Once they were, I was able to leave.

I had my six-week checkup scheduled, but did you think I was going back to her?! NOPE. I called around to find another doctor.

Sometime later, I received a phone call from a random, unknown number. I normally don't answer unknown numbers, but for some reason, I did this time, and IT WAS HER...MY OBSTETRICIAN!

I was shocked.

She began to apologize and say how sorry she was for what happened and sorry she didn't come to my room postpartum. She said she hadn't because she was "a mess" and didn't want to come in to face me and didn't want us to see her break down in my room. She hated that it happened like that… blah blah blah.

 All I could think was, "Mmhm mmhm mmhm."

She went on to explain what happened. I had developed chorioamnionitis, an infection in the amniotic cavity, and that's what pushed me into labor. She told me my placenta was sent away to be tested.

"So, what was that discharge I was having that you didn't send off?" I asked.
She confirmed it was from the infection.

Then she told me she understood if I didn't want to come back to her office and if I wanted someone else to do my six-week checkup.

I never spoke to her again.

I found a lawyer, signed contracts, and waited. The next thing I knew, I received a letter of declination with no explanation. When I called, I could never get in touch with the attorney. I wanted to drag my obstetrician through the slumps of the court–I still do– but it's too late. I had requested my whole medical report from the hospital and, whew! Not to mention the BILL! ! I wanted her to pay for ALLADAT!

I went to the new obstetrician who did my six-week checkup – my third obstetrician in three years. He asked a lot of questions regarding the recent happenings and did a lot of bloodwork. He even stated he would have delivered my baby instead of leaving my waters ruptured for that long. (I made sure that statement was available for the attorney, too).

When my results came back, he said he really didn't find anything definite to explain what happened but that he discovered I had a MTHFR gene mutation! A WHAT?! During my next pregnancy, I would need to be on Heparin, an anticoagulant, twice daily the entire pregnancy and taking low-dose aspirin every day leading up to pregnancy... Sheesh!

My husband and I began trying again, and I asked the doctor to put me on the same hormonal treatment that had worked the last time. He wouldn't prescribe it at first because it is primarily used to treat breast cancer patients, but I knew what worked, and I was learning to speak up for myself. He wasn't about to waste my time. He did end up prescribing it, and it worked a second time. I became pregnant with our daughter.

I stayed with this obstetrician for some time, but his office was always packed. One time they scheduled an ultrasound appointment for me, and I waited there for four hours, sitting on the floor in the hallway, pregnant, only for them to tell me the ultrasound technician didn't work that day. I said, "Well, y'all should have told that to whoever scheduled me for this appointment!" before walking out and never going back.

Now I was on the search for my FOURTH obstetrician.

I was so sick of this!

I knew at this point I needed someone who was familiar with what I had been through, and so, I contacted one of the doctors that came to sit with me when I was first admitted. When I got under her care, I was in her office every two weeks from the jump! I finally felt like my doctor was taking care of me! I was taking the Heparin, and she also added weekly Makena shots to prevent preterm labor.

Later in the pregnancy, the doctor noticed the baby wasn't growing as she should. So, I had to go to ANOTHER SPECIALIST!! The specialist did a scan and told me, "I don't know why she sent you here. There is nothing wrong with you." But I found out later that they didn't know what they were talking about. When I told my obstetrician about it, she sent them a message advocating for me. I started seeing my doctor two or three times every week, and I made it to 35 weeks.

Then, I was at the hospital with my best friend while she was having her baby, and I told her husband that my stomach started hurting. He reassured me that he could care for my friend and that I should go get checked out. It turned out I was in early labor AGAIN. I was 3.5 cm dilated and had no clue. The medical team hooked me up and prepared me for labor, but by the morning, the labor stopped, so they sent me home.
The next few weeks were a mess with extended labor, and at 37 weeks, my senses started to go off again. I felt like I was feeling fluid again, and I asked my doctor to be checked. She saw me right away, and I didn't have any fluid loss, but a growth scan showed intrauterine growth restriction (IUGR), the baby's size had fallen below normal range.

My doctor said, "Go to the labor ward. Don't even go to your car. I'm going to come induce you." No preparation. Nothing. By the next morning, my daughter, Christiana, was born at 5lbs 1oz.

I BEAT IT! I DID it this time!! But the effects from the journey and CARELESSNESS of that awful woman SWALLOWED me the whole pregnancy! I was so mean. I was so protective. I was so guarded. And my husband, Chris, caught it ALL!! I felt so bad. Before I delivered Christiana, we started to see a therapist because I didn't want to risk those feelings continuing after I delivered and potentially turning into postpartum depression or postpartum anxiety. We saw her until after I delivered and then decided that she really wasn't helping. Fortunately, my hormones leveled out, and I was okay, or so I thought. I buried a lot, and life went on.

Months went by, and eventually, I'm back to having painful, heavy cycles! I had an episode of severe pain during one that sent me to the ER! They did nothing about it and just sent me home. I had symptoms for weeks, so I called my doctor, and she got right on it! I was scheduled for a laparoscopy, hysteroscopy, and D&C to check for endometriosis. I didn't have endometriosis, but I did have a polyp. I'm not sure how long it was there, and I think I was rather small, but she removed it anyway.

Afterward, my doctor removed the polyp, and my cycles returned and were way better! Who knew that was what I needed?!

In 2018, my husband and I began trying for another child. I took the Femara again, and it took a couple of months before it worked. But it eventually did. I became pregnant, and like before, started taking the Heparin and Makena shots. This time, however, I started having reactions to the Makena shots. I had to choose between stopping the shots and risking preterm labor again, or continuing and having reactions each time. I couldn't take the reactions, so I made the decision to stop the shots. Luckily, I made it to the full term, but what I wasn't expecting was such a dramatic hormonal shift. By the last month or two, I just couldn't take it anymore! I shut down completely from the world. I stayed home. I changed my number and only gave it to three people and stayed home. Eventually, the pregnancy wore me down so badly, I couldn't take it. I drank some castor oil, was in labor an hour later, and delivered our son Semaj at 5lbs 6oz the next day! (I'm not advising anyone to do this. Because I dilate early in pregnancy and have "irritable uterus," I knew it would work.) It was risky, I know, but I was just that bad off! I needed relief. The feelings were boiling, and I was about to erupt.

Immediately after delivering, I felt better. This pregnancy went way more smoothly. His weight was watched, but he was good. I guess I just have small babies.

A few months postpartum, however, my hormones shift even more. I talked to my doctor and she put me on medication. I went to the gym every day, and everything was starting to look up. I weaned off the medication after about two or three months, and I was good.

Then all of a sudden, I gained over ten pounds in what seemed to be a week or so. I was bummed! What happened? How did this happen? Then my hormones shifted again! Off and on and on and off! Was it the PCOS?! I tried to deal with it silently, and for a while I was good. I got into cosmetology school in January 2020, we sold our home in March, but then the world stopped with the COVID pandemic. My anxiety picked up, not because of COVID but because I am triggered by death. I lost a dear friend a couple of months later, and I spun out of control. It was then I knew I couldn't handle it myself anymore. I started going to therapy and have been going since then.

Between having Semaj and 2020, I was in and out of doctors' offices because my pituitary levels had not improved. They hadn't gotten worse, but they hadn't gotten better either. I had an MRI, saw an endocrinologist, a neurologist, an ophthalmologist, a hematologist (for the MTHFR gene mutation). It seemed as though the tumor was pressing on my optic nerve, which they had been telling me since it was found, and that could cause blindness if the tumor grew over the nerve. I was supposed to have a follow-up MRI, but because of COVID, I still have not been back.   Oops! I will have to be getting back to testing, but those medical bills… …tsk tsk tsk.

By the end of 2020, I was doing really well, so I was like, "Okay, it's time to get at it again," and my husband and I started trying for Baby #3 (but really #4.) At my doctor's appointment in June, I had asked for the same fertility medications so that we could use them when we were ready. We tried the first few months without medication just to see if it would work naturally. But in September, nothing. October, nothing. November, nothing. And December, nothing. So, in January, I started taking the Femara.

Shortly after I started taking the medication, I had a dream that I was almost dying. In the dream, I was taking some medication, and it was slowly cutting off my ability to breathe. I didn't know what the dream could have been about, so I just pushed it to the side. I did, however, mention to my doctor that I wished to be monitored during the whole process, that I was concerned about the weight I had gained and couldn't lose among other things, and that I'd like my PCOS to be checked. I'm not sure if the message got to the doctor, but the nurse basically told me to wait and see.

I had been diagnosed with PCOS six years earlier in 2014, and I had totally forgotten all about it, so my doctor didn't have those records because I left them where they were. It was always on my mind but being that we never did anything for it, I just pushed it to the side. So, she told me she would check on my pituitary issue first and go from there. I agreed, and when my levels were checked, they came back normal for the first time in years! This was good news, but then we knew my symptoms weren't due to the pituitary gland. So maybe, it was the PCOS.

By February, I still heard nothing, so I'm referred BACK to my Reproductive Endocrinologist. I scheduled my appointment with him and brought up the PCOS. He reminded me that I was diagnosed with it back in 2014. So then I wondered if my diagnosis was based on observation or a complete workup. We paused on that.

March came, and I thought everything was going okay until BOOM! I was walking and had a very sharp pain extending down from my belly button. I thought nothing of it and just kept going with my daily routine. Later that night, I was extremely sleepy, so I went to bed early. Semaj was all over me, and I noticed my pelvic area was very sore, but it just felt like a normal cyst, which I'm used to and have had before.

I went to sleep and woke up the next morning feeling even sorer. When I looked at my belly while lying on my back, I noticed a bulge under my belly button that hurt when I touched it. I felt to see how big it was, and it felt huge.

I messaged my doctor, and they told me to come get checked. Turns out, I had a cyst the size of a grapefruit! My doctor told me to put everything on pause to hopefully avoid ovarian torsion, when the ovary twists over top the ligaments that support it.

That same day, my blood pressure was elevated and I was out of breath, over-exerted just from walking. I thought nothing of it, though, because I figured it was hot and I was moving a lot. The next day, my back and chest started hurting and I still felt breathless. The day after that, on my way to school, I thought I was about to pass out while driving. I was even more breathless, but this time with chest and shoulder pain. Everything felt like it was pushing upwards under my lungs.

I called the nurse right before the office closed and told her what I was feeling. She was able to schedule me in the next morning before the clinic opened. On the way to the appointment the next morning, I began to have EXTREME pain. I could barely drive myself to the doctor, but knew I needed to get there ASAP! When I got in, I had an ultrasound, and the cyst was even bigger. I would have to have surgery. I thought they meant maybe in the next week or so, but the next thing I knew, they were setting everything up, bringing me paperwork and directing me to the hospital where I would have surgery within an hour and a half.

It happened so fast! I didn't have time to think. So there I was, not sure how to feel. I felt physically great, but mentally I didn't know what was going on. But I did know my hormones were way off once again. I was so sensitive, crying about EVERYTHING, and just overall not myself!

The doctor explained that the cyst had started to leak out. Luckily, I was able to keep the ovary and just have the cyst removed. And that leaves me here where I am now: waiting to heal.

I know I live to tell my story to offer faith, hope, and commitment.
—*Yvonne McCombs*

A Mother's Day Loss

Yvonne McCombs

Silence strikes the room. "Honey, you need to go to the emergency room now." As everyone gazes at my lifeless baby on the sonogram. Clearly, this had to be a mistake, I convinced myself. When I get to the hospital, my baby will be alive and well. Along the car ride, I see billboards that affirm that Jesus loves me, which brings me much comfort. I thanked God in advance for the miracle!

I arrive at the hospital and am met with family, friends, and my pastor. We pray heaven down! Confessing The word of the Lord and binding up the enemy, we were not accepting that this baby had passed. I was encouraged! I am placed in a room with multiple moms who are connected to heart monitors as they loudly listen to their babies' heartbeats and chatter about how they didn't want kids, etc. I'm led to a bed covered by a curtain and a sonogram machine nearby. The ultrasound technician attempts to locate a heartbeat or movement from my baby but nothing. She then calls another nurse and by the looks on their faces, I can tell something is wrong. They open their mouth and say, "I'm sorry, we cannot locate a heartbeat." My world stood still, still holding onto faith, I ask if they can recheck. They rechecked two additional times and it was the same outcome. I am devastated. I am sent home to wait and see if a miracle could happen or "nature" could take its course. I am advised to follow up with my doctor.

A few weeks go by and I am at home unable to get comfortable. My stomach hurts extremely bad and changing positions is not making things better. I keep feeling pressure so assume I need to go to the restroom and then the unimaginable happens. My water breaks! I am only 4 months. My mom rushes me to the hospital and I am made to sit in the lobby to await a bed."" By this time, I am experiencing labor. My back is aching and I am having intense labor pains to the point I become afraid to stand because I know gravity can occur and this baby is coming out. After what seems like eternity, I'm called for vitals and I feel something slip out. I immediately tell my mom and we go to the restroom and my mother helps me and my baby lay lifeless on my pad. I am heartbroken. As thoughts flood my mind, my mom alerts the nurse who advises, "just put it in a cup." I'm too broken to react and I begin to lose a lot of blood. I still don't have a bed so I am not in the room but in the hallway. The blood loss causes me to feel dizzy and I begin blacking out. All I can remember is my mom being upset and them moving to get me in a room.

I finally make it into the room and start feeling the pressure in my abdomen again and when I stand up to get on the hospital bed, Plop! My placenta falls right on the floor, by this time I am numb. I am just being treated as another number. The medical staff is not concerned with me or my loss. I finally get discharged and was advised to follow up with my obgyn on Monday. The weekend passes and Monday is here. I have to get a vaginal exam to ensure all fetal tissue came out when my baby did. The obgyn says he sees some tissue and must get it out before it becomes infected. He then proceeds to pull at the tissue harshly while I cry telling him, "this hurts, you're hurting me." I ask him to stop and he eventually does. I leave my appointment. Not only did I experience pain from losing my baby, but physical and emotional pain. Those trained to take care of me acted as if I was another number and had very little compassion.

My first loss occurred in 2009, which will begin a ten-year span of 7 additional pregnancy losses. After my 6th loss, doctors began testing me to see what may be causing the losses, however all of my tests would come back negative. This is frustrating, and I want and need answers. During my 7th loss, I have a great team of doctors who did their best to get to the root of the issue, even going as far as developing a plan for when I try to conceive again. Sadly, I move and I am unable to keep this great team and the cycle began again with 2 additional losses and no answers. However, after my 8th loss, I vow to do things differently. Because I am a woman of faith, I do not believe that God would only allow me to birth death, so I cried out to him and imagined myself free falling into his huge arms and casting ALL of my cares on him. In Psalm 37:4, it says he will give you the desires of your heart and I stood and reminded God of that. I also continued to have several dreams affirming that one day I will birth a girl and a boy I had this dream repeatedly.

People said I should give up, adopt, no longer put my body through that, but I continued to stand on faith. I refuse to let my promise die and in 2019 I gave birth to two beautiful babies, a twin girl and a boy. I know I live to tell my story to offer faith, hope, and commitment. We may never know why God allows a thing, but we can always trust his love for us.

Undeserved Favor

Marenda Bullock Rose

When people get married or are young, the assumption is they'll have children whenever they decide to. This is not the case for 1 out of 6 couples who are diagnosed with infertility. It is also not true for 1 out of 4 pregnancies, which end in miscarriage. Howare these unfortunate occurrences so common and yet no one knows or talks about it? In particular, the onus is usually placed on women yet men are statistically just as responsible (both male and female factors each account for 40% of fertility challenges).

We were diagnosed with what accounts for the frustrating remaining 20%: unexplained infertility.

After the second miscarriage, we knew something may be wrong and began a fertility assessment along with exploring natural remedies. We were tested for everything—every genetic and cellular disorder, every physiological abnormality, every sperm and egg issue—and came back healthy in every way, though I would have rather received an answer. We were both taking <u>multiple supplements daily,</u> and I was also prescribed medications. After the third miscarriage, I needed to take a break. All the while, we were going on outwardly as though we had not lost three lives.

NATURAL CONCEPTION AFTER INFERTILITY
After the break and after a couple more months of trying with meds and supplements, I decided to stop all medications. The month I stopped the medications was the month we received our fourth positive test. ***We had conceived completely naturally without any interventions.***

I was distraught, in fear and exasperated that we would lose yet another baby. I couldn't for the life of me figure out why this was happening [yet]. I cried to God audibly and desperately, to the point where my husband had to come help me off the bathroom floor. But once that immediate emotional response was released, ***I had to remember everything I knew, not what I felt***. And everything I knew told me to get up. Moreover, the pregnancy continued to progress. Day after day.

EXTREME ANXIETY AFTER MULTIPLE MISCARRIAGES: TELLING THE ENEMY "NO"

In November, while attending a family member's funeral, I began to hemorrhage profusely. As my family members gathered around me in the bathroom, I cried again, confused at losing a fourth baby when my husband was sure God had promised us this one would make it. Was my lack of faith to blame, then? At the ER later that day, my husband and I prepared for bad news. There had been a hemorrhage, yes. But the baby was still alive with a strong heartbeat.

Besides being physically sick in my first trimester—which is fine because that's normal—I came to realize that despite the good news, despite the life I was carrying, the enemy was working overtime on my mind.
Due to the very graphic visuals of my miscarriages that kept replaying in my mind and the constant anxiety of what felt like impending loss, I was beginning to have nightmares. On the second night of my nightmares, I woke up in the middle of the night shaken but angry.

I was angry that my mind was being attacked like it was. We prayed, and we declared that I would NOT be tormented any longer. It was 4:19 AM, during the Fourth Watch, the same hour Jesus had seen his terrified disciples being tossed by a storm in their ship on the sea, and went out to comfort them. I was instantly comforted knowing that my Savior had seen me the entire time and had come to me in the Fourth Watch to help me pull myself up out of doubt. Reasonable doubt, considering the circumstances, but doubt all the same.

The nightmares stopped immediately. I am consciously and actively—and usually out loud—putting away anxiety when it tries to appear, as explicitly directed in Philippians 4:6-8. I remind myself daily that this is a new pregnancy and to look forward instead of backward. George's faith and reassurance was amazing and I look to his leadership often.

UNDESERVED FAVOR

In the infertility community, to be pregnant with a viable pregnancy in under one year is uncommon. However, by calculations, this child was conceived on October 20, *the same Sunday my pastor preached about being moved to the front of the line.* And we don't believe in coincidences! We wholly believe we have been moved to the front of the line, and I'm gonna tell it every chance I get.

I started being vocal about infertility online because infertility and miscarriages are so common but so little talked about because people are always asking, "when are you having children?" without thought that the person they're asking may have lost pregnancies or be infertile because infertility is a medical condition like diabetes or heart disease and should be treated as such, and chiefly because there is way too much dismal sadness and not enough hope and joy surrounding this topic.

We were blessed to eventually conceive a viable pregnancy but even if that weren't the case, there is still life and joy and gratefulness to God. And there are also other avenues for growing a family. That's the message I want to convey. I made a vow to God that anytime I talk about our pregnancy and this baby, *I will tell the full story* to glorify Him and help others.

CONTINUED ADVOCATE FOR INFERTILITY AWARENESS
For all out there who believe in the power of prayer, please pray for us and the health of our rainbow baby and my mind. Though pregnancy is behind me, and my son is now six weeks old, this story is really just beginning. I will continue to be an infertility ambassador, spreading awareness, acceptance, and confidence about this medical condition, sharing the methods and tips I feel helped us naturally, and being a living advocate of the joy and contentment Jesus can provide even in the face of great challenges beyond our control.

Speaking of control, something tells me I may want to loosen a grip on my need for that going forward. As surreal as it is, a tiny—and pretty demanding—human is here.

Caterpillar Dreams

Melaina Williams

Bedtime comes and my Prayers plead
with me for one more read.
The Very Hungry Little Caterpillar.
One prayer laid across my lap listening,
the other over my shoulder looking,
dissecting the final picture of the butterfly;
all yellows and purples and blues and red dotted.

A goodnight kiss to jelly cheeks
nudges my swollen heart
   REMEMBER?

My Prayers were only breath and syllables and tears
sewn together on the bathroom floor.
My stomach, though positioned with organs
still felt the hollow depths of longing
for a caterpillar who turns to butterfly,
who turns to rib kicks at the sip of cold water.

The longing. I know it well;
the blood-stained tissue on Mother's Day,
the altar calls for an open womb,
the sex positions for a titled uterus,
the prodding of a fibroid riddled body.
I know the dark days of a barren woman
I know the salted tears, I know the rage,
I know fear, something like a boa constrictor.

I also know the faith.
I know the fire tongues of women who call life forth.
I know how to wrestle with angels
I know how to retreat back to myself,
I know how to stand in the presence of whispers;
the haunts of those who dare to dream.

I know the voice of God.
Sounds a lot like me
when I'm only eating what has grown from the ground,
drinking water, present and grateful
—especially in the days of longing.
I know an empty womb is still blessed.

I know the faith that still believes.
Six years.
I shouted on the seventh
for my caterpillar had come and turned
butterfly
and that butterfly to kick,
with a soul ready to soar.
    REMEMBER.

I close the door as they nestle under their blankets.
My God, I swear I can hear the flutter
of their wings as they drift off to sleep.